PRAYERS
of POPE
FRANCIS

Foreword by Cardinal Michael Czerny, SJ
Introduction by Donna Orsuto
Edited by Cindy Wooden

UNITED STATES CONFERENCE OF CATHOLIC BISHOPS

Excerpts from Vatican text copyright © 2020 Libreria Editrice Vaticana, Vatican City State. All rights reserved. Used with permission.

Cover photo: CNS/Paul Haring.

ISBN 978-1-60137-679-4

First Printing, November 2020

Contents

Foreword

"Teach Us to Pray"

Jesus was praying in a certain place, and when he had finished, one of his disciples said to him, "Lord, teach us to pray just as John taught his disciples." (Luke 11:1)

With the Psalms and other great prayers of their Jewish tradition, the disciples were already well-supplied. Why ask Jesus for more instructions on prayer?

That unnamed disciple may have felt the need for something more here-and-now than the familiar, time-honored texts. Like all of us, he longed for something particular, personal, relevant. He wanted to commune with God as he saw Jesus doing.

Jesus satisfied the disciple's need, and ours, by suggesting prayer imbued with his own relationship with God, beginning with "Abba" which is probably closer to "Dad" than "Father":

This is how you are to pray: "Our Father in heaven, hallowed be your name, your kingdom come, your will be done, on earth as in heaven. Give us today our daily bread; and forgive us our debts, as we forgive our debtors; and do not subject us to the final test, but deliver us from the evil one." (Matthew 6:9-13)

If you or I now make the same request as that disciple, despite having the "Our Father" and so many other magnificent prayers, it could be to go from not praying to praying, from praying poorly to praying better in our here-and-now.

Today we can ask Pope Francis to "teach us to pray" as this volume brilliantly shows.

It's no surprise that he teaches and practices particular ways of praying. His praying embraces God in our times and our times in God. It expresses the importance of real needs—not my "wants," but more and more, the real needs of so many of our brothers and sisters. It offers readiness and willingness to cooperate in God's plan for the Church and the world.

The Pope revealed some of his prayer habits to pilgrims gathered in a sunny St. Peter's Square in June 2016: "In the evening, before going to bed, I pray this short prayer: 'Lord, if you will, you can make me clean' (Luke 5:12). And I pray five 'Our Fathers,' one for each of Jesus' wounds, because Jesus has cleansed us by his wounds." He spends the last hour of his day before the Blessed Sacrament, and he practices popular devotions like Our Lady Untier of Knots and the Sleeping St. Joseph.

The content of the Pope's praying connects him to the deepest concerns of our world today. During the first two months the 2020 pandemic, Pope Francis accompanied the people every day in prayer at the morning Mass in Santa Marta. His deep, existential prayer attracted countless participants, especially those who were suffering, the world over via live broadcasts.

He prayed for the elderly, for those who lost their work, for families in need and hungry; for those who are afraid or have lost a loved one; and for those who ensure the functioning of society—in the pharmacies, the supermarkets, transportation, the forces of order, and the overlooked like those who clean the hospitals and collect the rubbish. This daily prayer expressed his closeness to God and to ordinary people's daily lives. It moved the hearts of many. (See *clicktopray.org* and *www.popesprayer.va/prayfortheworld*.)

But praying, either in words spoken out loud or quietly whispered inside, is not our ultimate call: "We are all called to be holy by living our lives with love and by bearing witness in everything we do, wherever we find ourselves." Prayer leads to life and action. For "I do not believe in holiness without prayer, even though that prayer need not be lengthy or involve intense emotions" (*Gaudete et exsultate*, nos. 14, 147). Doing and praying are intertwined. Beautiful, prayerful, every-day, active holiness is illustrated over and over in these pages.

What about when words seem to get in the way? Pope Francis shows and teaches non-verbal forms of prayer, too. Consider this passage from *Laudato si'* (no. 97). Try to "see" it as you read it:

> The Lord was able to invite others to be attentive to the beauty that there is in the world because he himself was in constant touch with nature, lending it an attention full of fondness and wonder. As he made his way throughout the land, he often stopped to contemplate the beauty sown by his Father, and invited his disciples to perceive a divine message in things: "Lift up your eyes, and see how the fields are already white for harvest" (*Jn* 4:35).

Touch, attention, wonder, beauty, a divine message: here the Holy Father shows us how to let the surrounding world invite us to pray.

Pope Francis often asks us to exercise our imagination to place ourselves in a particular scene with Jesus, with Mary or the disciples. This technique, suggested by St. Ignatius of Loyola, founder of the Jesuit Order, creates a space where seeds of prayer can grow—seeds that we find throughout his writings.

Pope Francis prays for and with us; encourages us to pray; and teaches and shows us how to pray. And so, with Pope Francis, let us pray.

Cardinal Michael Czerny S.J.
Undersecretary, Migrants and Refugees Section
Dicastery for Promoting Integral Human Development

INTRODUCTION

I still remember the buzz in St. Peter's Square March 13, 2013, when Pope Francis appeared for the first time on the loggia of the Basilica. Along with thousands of others, my friends and I were packed into the square. Amazingly, though it seemed impossible to move an inch in any direction, when the door from the loggia opened, we were all swept forward about ten feet.

After greeting the crowd simply in Italian with the words "Brothers and sisters, good evening," he began his pontificate, in a surprising way, with three brief moments of public prayer.

His first invitation was to *pray with him* for Pope Emeritus Benedict XVI, "that the Lord may bless him and that Our Lady may keep him." Pope Francis and the people gathered prayed aloud in Italian three simple well-known prayers: Our Father, Hail Mary, and Glory Be.

He then spoke of the journey that he, as the new bishop of Rome, and the people of the city were about to embark upon and invited those present to join him to "always pray for one another" and "for the whole world, that there may be a great spirit of fraternity."

He concluded by asking us *to pray for him*: "Before the bishop blesses his people, I ask you to pray to the Lord that he will bless me: the prayer of the people asking the blessing for their bishop. Let us make, in silence, this prayer: your prayer over me."

It seemed impossible that such a boisterous crowd could enter into such intense silence, but upon his humble and sincere request we did; the hush over the crowd was instant and we silently and fervently prayed for our new pope and bishop of Rome.

These three ways of praying—a simple prayer for a specific person using vocal prayers familiar to us all, an invitation to pray for one another and for the world, recognizing that we are all connected to one another as brothers and sisters, and finally a request that the people pray for him—offer a poignant insight into what underlies this pontificate and the content that you will find in *Prayers of Pope Francis*.

Prayers of a Pontifex

The prayers selected for this volume reveal a pastor who stands with the people, who intercedes with them and for them.

During a General Audience on June 17, 2020, Pope Francis explained how the prophet Moses was a "bridge" and "intercessor," the example of a leader who "never forgets his people."

"What a beautiful example for all pastors who must be bridges," he said. "This is why they are called *pontifex*, bridges. Pastors are the bridges between the people they belong to and to God, to whom they belong by vocation." Of course, the *pontifex*, par excellence, he continued, is Jesus, who is "the bridge between us and the Father. And Jesus intercedes for us; he shows the Father the wounds that are the price of our salvation, and he intercedes."

However, pastors, like the Hebrew prophets, are not perfect, which is one reason Pope Francis unfailingly asks for prayers for himself whenever possible, such as at the end of every Angelus and in meetings with individuals and groups. He recognizes that he is a sinner, like everyone else, who is both "mercy'd" and called by God to serve.[1] This is why both personal prayer rooted in the honest acknowledgement of weakness and sin and the prayerful support of others are important for him.

Pope Francis prays as a Christian. Christian prayer is rooted in a personal encounter with Jesus Christ, who through the working of the Holy Spirit leads us to an experience of God as Abba, Father. As he explained in his catechesis on May 13, in prayer we "place ourselves into the merciful arms of God," where we can "feel enveloped by that mystery of happiness which is Trinitarian life, to feel like guests who were not worthy of so much honor." Time spent in personal prayer allows one to enter more fully into an intimate and personal relationship with the One who loves us unconditionally.

Personal Prayer and Public Prayer

Without a doubt, Pope Francis's personal prayer influences his public prayer. One might ask, what does his daily

---

1. Pope Francis's motto, *Miserando atque eligendo,* is a reference to a passage from the Venerable St. Bede: "Jesus saw the tax collector and, because he saw him through the eyes of mercy and chose him, he said to him: Follow me" (with reference to Matthew 9:9-13). In remarking that this passage is from the daily reading of October 21 for the feast of St. Matthew, Austin Ivereigh notes that this feast day is "the day in 1953 when the young Jorge Mario was 'mercy'd' by God in the confessional of the basilica in Flores." See Austin Ivereigh, *The Great Reformer. Francis and the Making of a Radical Pope,* p. 222.

personal prayer look like? He has said that it consists of the breviary, Mass, the rosary, and one hour of adoration before the Blessed Sacrament. He takes opportunities to pray silently throughout the day, "even", he says, "when I am waiting at the dentist or at other times of the day."

Pope Francis also incorporates the role of memory in prayer. In his 2013 interview with Antonio Spadaro, "A Big Heart Open to God" in *America* magazine, he explained,

> Prayer for me is always a prayer full of memory, of recollection, even the memory of my own history or what the Lord has done in his church or in a particular parish. For me it is the memory of which St. Ignatius speaks in the first week of the Exercises in the encounter with the merciful Christ crucified. And I ask myself: "What have I done for Christ? What am I doing for Christ? What should I do for Christ?"…But above all, I also know that the Lord remembers me. I can forget about him, but I know he never, ever forgets me.…It is this memory that makes me his son and that makes me a father, too.

In Pope Francis's description of his personal life of prayer, three points become clear. First, his prayers are shaped by his Catholic faith: he prays as many Catholics do with the Liturgy of the Hours, the rosary, eucharistic adoration, and moments of mental prayer, all of these culminating in daily Mass. Second, he prays as a Jesuit who is rooted in the spirituality of the spiritual exercises of St. Ignatius, pivoting, first on an encounter with Christ crucified, who manifests God's mercy and encourages him to reflect on his response to this outpouring of love, and then on the "Contemplation for experiencing Divine Love," which begins with a remembrance of God who is the giver of all good gifts and ends with a prayer of surrender and trust, the "Suscipe": "Take Lord receive my memory, my understanding, my entire will . . ." In his personal life and in his pontificate, Pope Francis recognizes that God is always quick to reach out to us first. "Dios te primerea," as he likes to say.[2] Finally, Pope Francis hints at how the memory in prayer of his filial relationship with a merciful and all-loving God informs his own personal vocation as a priest.

Prayer Beyond Boundaries

Pope Francis's commitment to ecumenical and interreligious dialogue is well-known, though less known is his prayer in an ecumenical and interreligious context.

With regard to prayer with other Christians, Pope Francis has reiterated the irrevocable commitment of the Catholic Church to promote Christian unity. (See his May 24 letter on the 25th anniversary of *Ut Unum Sint.*) He is convinced that Christians can and must pray and work together for the common good. An example of this prayer was when, on the solemnity of the Annunciation this year, he invited Christian leaders around the world to pray together the Our Father as a way to implore God to end the pandemic.

As this collection of prayers demonstrates, he has prayed on numerous occasions in the presence of people of other religions. In June 2014, for instance, Jewish and Muslim political and religious leaders joined him in the Vatican to pray for peace in the Holy Land.

---

2. Ivereigh, p.13.

During the COVID-19 pandemic, Pope Francis readily embraced the proposal of the High Committee for Human Fraternity for a worldwide day of prayer, fasting and acts of charity. A more profound understanding of his openness to this proposal is gained by being aware of his conviction that deep in the heart of every person there is a voice crying out to God.

"We all have this voice within," he said at his General Audience on May 6. "A voice that comes forth spontaneously without anyone commanding it, a voice that asks itself about the meaning of our journey on earth, especially when we find ourselves in darkness."

Pope Francis is convinced that "prayer belongs to everyone: to men and women of every religion, and probably also to those who profess none." It arises from the human heart. (See his General Audience on May 13.) As he explains, the cry of prayer is "chiseled in all of creation. Everything invokes and implores, so that the mystery of mercy may be definitively fulfilled." (See General Audience on May 6.)

At the end of his landmark encyclical *Laudato si'*, he offers two prayers: one for those who believe in God "the all-powerful Creator" and one for Christians who "take up the commitment of creation" offered by "the Gospel of Jesus." As he explains at one of his May 13 General Audience catecheses on prayer, "The prayer of a Christian arises from a revelation. . . . It was Jesus who revealed God to us."

Devotion to the Blessed Virgin Mary

Pope Francis's Marian piety is also evident throughout this volume.

On the first morning of his pontificate, Pope Francis went to the Basilica of St. Mary Major to pray silently before one of the oldest and most venerated icons of Mary who is represented holding the child Jesus tenderly in her arms. The icon is the Salus Populi Romani, whose name translates literally as "salvation, or health, of the Roman people". As archbishop of Buenos Aires, he had regularly stopped there on each of his previous visits to Rome. Still today, he goes there to pray before and after every apostolic journey. Mary has been a companion for Romans on their journeys for centuries: in good times and in bad. Clearly, Pope Francis sees her as a silent companion on his apostolic journeys and present especially in times of crisis, as at the height of the COVID-19 lockdown in Italy, when the icon was brought to St. Peter's Square for the extraordinary prayer on March 27, 2020. The simplicity of this Marian devotion along with others, including that of Mary Undoer of Knots, Our Lady of Aparecida, and Our Lady of Silence, points to a quiet and deep trust that she is a powerful intercessor before her Son, Jesus Christ. His experience of the Blessed Virgin Mary's "maternal, tender and steadfast presence" spills over into his formal prayers as pope.

As you read this volume, stopping to meditate on one prayer or another, *pray with him* for the Church, for the world, for suffering humanity, recognizing that the lives of all men and women throughout the world, and indeed with the whole of creation, are woven together in the tapestry of God's love. Remember also to *pray for him*.

Donna Orsuto
Professor, Institute of Spirituality, Pontifical Gregorian University, and Director of the Lay Centre at Foyer Unitas (www.laycentre.org) in Rome

PRAYERS TO CONCLUDE
MAJOR DOCUMENTS

Popes traditionally close major documents with a brief prayer to Mary, and Pope Francis has continued that practice of entrusting to the Mother of Jesus the special intentions raised in his documents. But he often goes further, using those closing prayers to present his concerns in a new, more lyrical form, and giving Catholics a way to share the needs closest to his heart and bring them to God.

In fact, Pope Francis wrote two prayers to conclude his encyclical *Fratelli Tutti*: one that could be used by anyone who believes in God as creator of the world and of all people, and another specifically for Christians. The encyclical, calling all people of goodwill to recognize their common humanity and build a world where each person is valued, contained critiques of the ways people and their political systems ignore, wound or discard people. The prayers not only ask for God's help to remedy those situations, but remind believers that they, too, have a responsibility to take steps to do so.

The first invocation is called "A Prayer to the Creator":

Lord, Father of our human family,
you created all human beings equal in dignity:
pour forth into our hearts a fraternal spirit
and inspire in us a dream of renewed encounter,
dialogue, justice and peace.
Move us to create healthier societies
and a more dignified world,
a world without hunger, poverty, violence and war.

May our hearts be open
to all the peoples and nations of the earth.
May we recognize the goodness and beauty
that you have sown in each of us,
and thus forge bonds of unity, common projects,
and shared dreams. Amen.

The second prayer, he titled "An Ecumenical Christian Prayer":

O God, Trinity of love,
from the profound communion of your divine life,
pour out upon us a torrent of fraternal love.
Grant us the love reflected in the actions of Jesus,
in his family of Nazareth,
and in the early Christian community.

Grant that we Christians may live the Gospel,
discovering Christ in each human being,
recognizing him crucified
in the sufferings of the abandoned

and forgotten of our world,
and risen in each brother or sister
who makes a new start.

Come, Holy Spirit, show us your beauty,
reflected in all the peoples of the earth,
so that we may discover anew
that all are important and all are necessary,
different faces of the one humanity
that God so loves. Amen.

At the end of *Querida Amazonia*, his 2020 apostolic exhortation reflecting on the themes of the 2019 Synod of Bishops for the Amazon, Pope Francis wrote that after using the document to share "a few of my dreams" for the region and recognizing the human and environmental marvels of the region, it felt right to turn in prayer to Mary, who is particularly dear to Catholics in the region.

The prayer praises Mary as the mother of Jesus and mother of his disciples, asks her to protect the people and the nature God created, acknowledges the pain she experiences when her children suffer and requests her help in converting the hearts of those who would destroy human communities and natural resources simply in a search for profit.

Here is the prayer:

Mother of life,
in your maternal womb Jesus took flesh,
the Lord of all that exists.
Risen, he transfigured you by his light
and made you the Queen of all creation.

For that reason, we ask you, Mary, to reign
in the beating heart of Amazonia.

Show yourself the Mother of all creatures,
in the beauty of the flowers, the rivers,
the great river that courses through it
and all the life pulsing in its forests.
Tenderly care for this explosion of beauty.

Ask Jesus to pour out all his love
on the men and women who dwell there,
that they may know how to appreciate and care for it.

Bring your Son to birth in their hearts,
so that he can shine forth in the Amazon region,
in its peoples and in its cultures,
by the light of his word,
by his consoling love,
by his message of fraternity and justice.

And at every Eucharist,
may all this awe and wonder be lifted up
to the glory of the Father.

Mother, look upon the poor of the Amazon region,
for their home is being destroyed by petty interests.
How much pain and misery,
how much neglect and abuse there is
in this blessed land
overflowing with life!

Touch the hearts of the powerful,
for, even though we sense that the hour is late,

you call us to save
what is still alive.

Mother whose heart is pierced,
who yourself suffer in your mistreated sons and
     daughters,
and in the wounds inflicted on nature,
reign in the Amazon,
together with your Son.
Reign so that no one else can claim lordship
over the handiwork of God.

We trust in you, Mother of life.
Do not abandon us
in this dark hour.

Amen.

Pope Francis's 2016 exhortation, *Amoris Laetitia* (*The Joy of Love*), made headlines for its treatment of ministry to Catholics who had been divorced and civilly remarried. But that issue was only a small portion of the long document, which discussed the full gamut of issues related to family life—from engagement and marriage preparation to retirement and grandparenting. Looking honestly at the challenges and problems facing many families, the document also sang the joys and praises of family life.

At the end of the document, Pope Francis made the obvious choice of entrusting the world's families to the care of the Holy Family—Jesus, Mary and Joseph—who also experienced the joys and heartaches of family life.

Prayer to the Holy Family

Jesus, Mary and Joseph,
in you we contemplate
the splendor of true love;
to you we turn with trust.

Holy Family of Nazareth,
grant that our families too
may be places of communion and prayer,
authentic schools of the Gospel
and small domestic churches.

Holy Family of Nazareth,
may families never again experience violence, rejection
    and division;
may all who have been hurt or scandalized
find ready comfort and healing.

Holy Family of Nazareth,
make us once more mindful
of the sacredness and inviolability of the family, and its
    beauty in God's plan.
Jesus, Mary and Joseph,
Graciously hear our prayer.

Amen.

At the end of *Laudato Si'*, his landmark encyclical on "integral ecology"—protecting human beings and the natural environment—Pope Francis included two separate prayers. While profoundly Christian and building on concepts from Catholic social teaching, the 2015 encyclical called on all people to accept their shared responsibility for the Earth and for everyone and everything that lives on it.

For that reason, Pope Francis wrote, he included two prayers; "the first we can share with all who believe in a God who is the all-powerful Creator, while in the other we Christians ask for inspiration to take up the commitment to creation set before us by the Gospel of Jesus."

A Prayer for Our Earth

All-powerful God, you are present in the whole universe
and in the smallest of your creatures.
You embrace with your tenderness all that exists.
Pour out upon us the power of your love,
that we may protect life and beauty.
Fill us with peace, that we may live
as brothers and sisters, harming no one.
O God of the poor,
help us to rescue the abandoned and forgotten of
    this earth,
so precious in your eyes.
Bring healing to our lives,
that we may protect the world and not prey on it,
that we may sow beauty, not pollution and destruction.
Touch the hearts
of those who look only for gain
at the expense of the poor and the earth.
Teach us to discover the worth of each thing,
to be filled with awe and contemplation,
to recognize that we are profoundly united
with every creature

as we journey towards your infinite light.
We thank you for being with us each day.
Encourage us, we pray, in our struggle
for justice, love and peace.

A Christian Prayer in Union with Creation

Father, we praise you with all your creatures.
They came forth from your all-powerful hand;
they are yours, filled with your presence and your tender
    love.
Praise be to you!

Son of God, Jesus,
through you all things were made.
You were formed in the womb of Mary our Mother,
you became part of this earth,
and you gazed upon this world with human eyes.
Today you are alive in every creature
in your risen glory.
Praise be to you!

Holy Spirit, by your light
you guide this world towards the Father's love
and accompany creation as it groans in travail.
You also dwell in our hearts
and you inspire us to do what is good.
Praise be to you!

Triune Lord, wondrous community of infinite love,
teach us to contemplate you
in the beauty of the universe,

for all things speak of you.
Awaken our praise and thankfulness
for every being that you have made.
Give us the grace to feel profoundly joined
to everything that is.

God of love, show us our place in this world
as channels of your love
for all the creatures of this earth,
for not one of them is forgotten in your sight.
Enlighten those who possess power and money
that they may avoid the sin of indifference,
that they may love the common good, advance the weak,
and care for this world in which we live.
The poor and the earth are crying out.
O Lord, seize us with your power and light,
help us to protect all life,
to prepare for a better future,
for the coming of your Kingdom
of justice, peace, love and beauty.
Praise be to you!

Amen.

About nine months after his election to succeed Pope
Benedict XVI, Pope Francis published *The Joy of the Gospel*,
a call for Catholics to become "missionary disciples" and a
comprehensive presentation of the priorities of his ministry
as successor of St. Peter.

Starting from the papal tradition of a final paragraph
entrusting the intentions of the document to Mary, Pope

Francis offered her as a model and example of that missionary disciple he was calling all Catholics to be: one committed to "the revolutionary nature of love and tenderness," strong enough to put others first and to work for justice, wise enough to see God at work in all things and open enough to work for a church that reaches out to and welcomes all people.

Mary, Virgin and Mother,
you who, moved by the Holy Spirit,
welcomed the word of life
in the depths of your humble faith:
as you gave yourself completely to the Eternal One,
help us to say our own "yes"
to the urgent call, as pressing as ever,
to proclaim the good news of Jesus.

Filled with Christ's presence,
you brought joy to John the Baptist,
making him exult in the womb of his mother.
Brimming over with joy,
you sang of the great things done by God.
Standing at the foot of the cross
with unyielding faith,
you received the joyful comfort of the resurrection,
and joined the disciples in awaiting the Spirit
so that the evangelizing Church might be born.

Obtain for us now a new ardor born of the resurrection,
that we may bring to all the Gospel of life
which triumphs over death.
Give us a holy courage to seek new paths,

that the gift of unfading beauty
may reach every man and woman.

Virgin of listening and contemplation,
Mother of love, Bride of the eternal wedding feast,
pray for the Church, whose pure icon you are,
that she may never be closed in on herself
or lose her passion for establishing God's kingdom.

Star of the new evangelization,
help us to bear radiant witness to communion,
service, ardent and generous faith,
justice and love of the poor,
that the joy of the Gospel
may reach to the ends of the earth,
illuminating even the fringes of our world.

Mother of the living Gospel,
wellspring of happiness for God's little ones,
pray for us.

Amen. Alleluia!

Pope Francis's first encyclical letter was actually a document begun by Pope Benedict XVI meant to close the 2012-13 Year of Faith and complete his trilogy of encyclicals on the theological virtues: love, hope, and faith. Pope Benedict had completed a first draft before resigning early in 2013, and Pope Francis picked up the text and completed it.

One obvious mark of Pope Francis's authorship was the prayer to Mary concluding the document:

Mother, help our faith!

Open our ears to hear God's word and to recognize his voice and call.

Awaken in us a desire to follow in his footsteps, to go forth from our own land and to receive his promise.

Help us to be touched by his love, that we may touch him in faith.

Help us to entrust ourselves fully to him and to believe in his love, especially at times of trial, beneath the shadow of the cross, when our faith is called to mature.

Sow in our faith the joy of the Risen One.

Remind us that those who believe are never alone.

Teach us to see all things with the eyes of Jesus, that he may be light for our path. And may this light of faith always increase in us, until the dawn of that undying day, which is Christ himself, your Son, our Lord!

CHAPTER 2

PRAYERS AT THE COLOSSEUM

During Holy Week—a week filled with powerful liturgies—thousands of people gather in the night at Rome's Colosseum on Good Friday to slowly, methodically remember Jesus' passion and death. Carrying candles, they are accompanied by professional speakers who announce each Station of the Cross, read the relevant scripture passages and proclaim meditations, which are drafted anew each year. Those contributions—from people chosen by the pope—often tie Christ's suffering to the painful experiences of modern men and women, who too often are the victims of war, natural disasters, unjust systems, abuse, exploitation or addiction.

Since St. Paul VI revived the liturgy at the Colosseum in 1964, popes have presided over the ceremony, usually giving a speech at the end to make explicit the connection between Christ's suffering and God's love for humanity yesterday, today and forever.

Pope Francis, though, has made it his tradition to offer a prayer at the end of the service, although he allowed silence to reign over St. Peter's Square when the service was moved there for Good Friday 2020, during the first wave of the COVID-19 pandemic.

For 2019, he had asked Italian Consolata Sister Eugenia Bonetti to write the meditations; she has dedicated her ministry to helping the victims of human trafficking and to educating the public about the ongoing reality of modern slavery.

At the end of the Via Crucis at the Colosseum, Pope Francis prayed:

Lord Jesus, help us to see in your Cross all the crosses of the world:

the cross of those who hunger for bread and for love;

the cross of those who are alone and abandoned, even by their own children and relatives,

the cross of those who thirst for justice and peace;

the cross of the elderly who bear the weight of the years and of solitude;

the cross of migrants who find doors closed due to fear, and hearts armored by political calculations;

the cross of the little ones, wounded in their innocence and their purity;

the cross of humanity that wanders in the darkness of uncertainty and in the obscurity of the culture of the momentary;

the cross of families broken by betrayal, by the seductions of the evil one or by murderous lightness and selfishness;

the cross of the consecrated who seek tirelessly to bring your light in the world and who feel rejected, mocked and humiliated;

the cross of the consecrated who along the way have forgotten their first love;

the cross of your children who, believing in you and seeking to live according to your word, find themselves marginalized and rejected even by their relatives and peers;

the cross of our weaknesses, of our hypocrisies, of our betrayals, of our sins and of our many broken promises;

the cross of your church who, faithful to your Gospel, struggles to bring your love even among the baptized themselves;

the cross of the church, your bride, who feels continually assailed from within and without;

the cross of our common home that withers gravely before our selfish eyes, blinded by greed and power.

Lord Jesus, revive in us the hope of the resurrection and of your definitive victory against every evil and every death. Amen!

For Good Friday 2018, Pope Francis had asked the editor

of *L'Osservatore Romano*, who was a high school religion teacher, to gather a group of his current and former students to write the meditations. Fifteen young people, ages 16 to 28, offered their reflections. At the end of the service, Pope Francis prayed:

Lord Jesus, our gaze is turned to you, full of shame, remorse and hope.

Before your supreme love

shame pervades us for having left you alone to suffer for our sins:

shame for having fled when tested despite having said to you a thousand times: "Even if all leave you, I will never leave you";

shame for having chosen Barabbas and not you, power and not you, appearances and not you, the god of money and not you, worldliness and not eternity;

shame for having tempted you with mouth and heart, each time that we faced a trial, saying to you: "You are the Messiah, save yourself and we will believe!";

shame because many people, and even some of your ministers, have allowed themselves to be deceived by ambition and vainglory, losing their dignity and the love they had at first;

shame because our generations are leaving young people a world fractured by divisions and war; a

world devoured by selfishness in which the young, the children, the sick, the elderly are marginalized;

shame for having lost our shame;

Lord Jesus, grant us always the grace of holy shame!

Our gaze is also filled with remorse which before your eloquent silence implores your mercy:

remorse which germinates in the certainty that you alone can save us from evil; you alone can heal us from our leprosy of hate, selfishness, pride, greed, vengeance, avarice, idolatry; you alone can embrace us again, restoring our filial dignity and rejoicing in our return to home, to life;

remorse which blossoms from feeling our pettiness, our nothingness, our vanity, and which allows itself to be caressed by your pleasing and powerful call to conversion;

remorse of David who, from the abyss of his misery, found in you his unique strength;

remorse which arises from our shame, which is born from the certainty that our heart will always be unsettled until we find you and in you its sole source of fulfillment and calm;

the remorse of Peter who, in meeting your gaze, wept bitterly for having denied you before men.

Lord Jesus, grant us always the grace of holy remorse!

Before your supreme majesty, in the obscurity of our despair, a glimmer of hope ignites because we know that your unique measure of loving us is that of loving us without measure:

hope because your message continues to inspire, still today, many people and peoples for whom good alone can conquer evil and cruelty; forgiveness alone can destroy rancor and vengeance; fraternal embrace alone can dispel hostility and fear of the other;

hope because your sacrifice continues, still today, to emit the perfume of divine love which caresses the hearts of many young people who continue to consecrate their lives to you, becoming living examples of charity and gratuitousness in this world of ours, devoured by the logic of profit and easy earnings;

hope because so many missionaries continue, still today, to challenge humanity's dormant conscience, risking their lives to serve you in the poor, the rejected, the immigrants, the invisible, the exploited, the hungry and the imprisoned;

hope because your church, holy and comprised of sinners, continues, still today, despite attempts to discredit her, to be a light that illuminates, encourages, comforts and witnesses to your boundless love for mankind, a model of altruism, an ark of salvation and font of certainty and truth;

hope because the Resurrection has sprung from your cross, fruit of the greed and cowardice of many doctors of

the Law and hypocrites, transforming the darkness of the tomb into the splendor of the dawn of the Sunday whose sun never sets, teaching us that your love is our hope.

Lord Jesus, grant us always the grace of holy hope!

Help us, Son of man, to strip ourselves of the arrogance of the robber placed at your left and of the shortsightedness of the corrupt, who have seen in you an opportunity to exploit, a condemned man to criticize, a defeated man to deride, another occasion to ascribe to others, and even to God, their own faults.

We ask you instead, Son of God, to identify us with the good robber who looked at you with eyes full of shame, remorse and hope; who, with the eyes of faith, saw divine victory in your seeming defeat and thus knelt before your mercy, and with honesty, stole paradise! Amen!

To write the 2017 meditations, Pope Francis asked Anne-Marie Pelletier, a French biblical scholar who is also a wife, mother and grandmother. She said she began work on the meditations without a specific theme, simply trying "to follow in the footsteps of Jesus as he went up to Golgotha." The end result, though, was a focus on how love is stronger than any form of evil or suffering. At the end of the service, Pope Francis prayed:

O Christ! Abandoned and betrayed even by your own and sold for next to nothing.

O Christ! Judged by sinners, handed over by those in authority.

O Christ! Suffering in the flesh, crowned with thorns and clothed in purple. O Christ! Mocked and mercilessly nailed to the cross.

O Christ! Rent by the lance that pierced your heart.

O Christ! Dead and buried, you who are the God of life and of existence.

O Christ! Our only savior, we turn to you this year too with eyes lowered in shame and hearts filled with hope:

Ashamed of all the scenes of devastation, destruction and drowning that have become a normal part of our lives;

Ashamed of the innocent blood shed daily of women, children, migrants and people persecuted because of the color of their skin or their ethnic and social diversity or because of their faith in you;

Ashamed of the too many times that, like Judas and Peter, we have sold you and betrayed you and left you alone to die for our sins, fleeing like cowards from our responsibilities;

Ashamed of our silence before injustices; for our reticence in giving and greed in grabbing and conquering; for our high-pitched defense of our interests and timid defense of other's; for our alacrity in following the path of evil and apathy when it comes to following the path of good;

Ashamed of all the times that we bishops, priests, consecrated men and women have been a cause of scandal and wound to your body, the church; for having forgotten our first love, our initial enthusiasm and total availability, letting our hearts and our consecration rust.

So much shame Lord, but our hearts also feel nostalgia for the confident hope that you will not treat us according to our merits but solely according to the abundance of your mercy; that our betrayal does not diminish the immensity of your love; your maternal and paternal heart does not forget us because of the hardness of our own;

The certain hope that our names are etched on your heart and that we are set in the pupil of your eyes;

The hope that your cross may transform our hardened hearts into hearts of flesh that are able to dream, to forgive and to love; that it may transform this dark night of your cross into the brilliant dawn of your Resurrection;

The hope that your faithfulness is not based on our own;

The hope that the hosts of men and women who are faithful to your cross may continue to abide in fidelity, just as yeast gives flavor and as light reveals new horizons in the body of our wounded humanity;

The hope that your church will seek to be the voice that cries in the wilderness of humanity in order to prepare the way for your triumphant return, when you will come to judge the living and the dead;

The hope that good will be victorious despite its apparent defeat!

O Lord Jesus! Son of God, innocent victim of our ransom, before your royal banner, before the mystery of your death and glory, before your [executioner's] scaffold, we kneel in shame and hope and we ask that you bathe us in the blood and water that flowed from your lacerated heart; to forgive our sins and our faults;

We ask you to remember our brethren crushed by violence, indifference and war;

We ask you to break the chains that keep us imprisoned in our selfishness, our willful blindness and, in the vanity of our worldly calculations.

O Christ! We ask you to teach us never to be ashamed of your cross, not to exploit it but to honor and worship it, because with it you have shown us the horror of our sins, the greatness of your love, the injustice of our decisions and the power of your mercy. Amen.

For Good Friday 2016, Pope Francis tapped Italian Cardinal Gualtiero Bassetti of Perugia-Citta della Pieve, who focused on modern families and situations that cause them to suffer. Pope Francis ended the nighttime service by praying:

O Cross of Christ, symbol of divine love and of human injustice, icon of the supreme sacrifice for love and of boundless selfishness even unto madness, instrument of death and the way of resurrection, sign of obedience and emblem of betrayal, the gallows of persecution and the banner of victory.

O Cross of Christ, today too we see you raised up in our sisters and brothers killed, burned alive, throats slit and decapitated by barbarous blades amid cowardly silence.

O Cross of Christ, today too we see you in the faces of children, of women and people, worn out and fearful, who flee from war and violence and who often only find death and many Pilates who wash their hands.

O Cross of Christ, today too we see you in those filled with knowledge and not with the spirit, scholars of death and not of life, who instead of teaching mercy and life, threaten with punishment and death, and who condemn the just.

O Cross of Christ, today too we see you in unfaithful ministers who, instead of stripping themselves of their own vain ambitions, divest even the innocent of their dignity.

O Cross of Christ, today too we see you in the hardened hearts of those who easily judge others, with hearts

ready to condemn even to the point of stoning, without ever recognizing their own sins and faults.

O Cross of Christ, today too we see you in expressions of fundamentalism and in terrorist acts committed by followers of some religions which profane the name of God and which use the holy name to justify their unprecedented violence.

O Cross of Christ, today too we see you in those who wish to remove you from public places and exclude you from public life, in the name of a pagan laicism or that equality you yourself taught us.

O Cross of Christ, today too we see you in the powerful and in arms dealers who feed the cauldron of war with the innocent blood of our brothers and sisters and feed their children with bread drenched in blood.

O Cross of Christ, today too we see you in traitors who, for thirty pieces of silver, would consign anyone to death.

O Cross of Christ, today too we see you in thieves and corrupt officials who, instead of safeguarding the common good and morals, sell themselves in the despicable marketplace of immorality.

O Cross of Christ, today too we see you in the foolish who build warehouses to store up treasures that perish, leaving Lazarus to die of hunger at their doorsteps.

O Cross of Christ, today too we see you in the destroyers of our "common home," who by their selfishness ruin the future of coming generations.

O Cross of Christ, today too we see you in the elderly who have been abandoned by their families, in the disabled and in children starving and cast-off by our egotistical and hypocritical society.

O Cross of Christ, today too we see you in the Mediterranean and Aegean Seas which have become insatiable cemeteries, reflections of our indifferent and anesthetized conscience.

O Cross of Christ, image of love without end and way of the Resurrection, today too we see you in noble and upright persons who do good without seeking praise or admiration from others.

O Cross of Christ, today too we see you in ministers who are faithful and humble, who illuminate the darkness of our lives like candles that burn freely in order to brighten the lives of the least among us.

O Cross of Christ, today too we see you in the faces of consecrated women and men—good Samaritans—who have left everything to bind up, in evangelical silence, the wounds of poverty and injustice.

O Cross of Christ, today too we see you in the merciful who have found in mercy the greatest expression of justice and faith.

O Cross of Christ, today too we see you in simple men and women who live their faith joyfully day in and day out, in filial observance of your commandments.

O Cross of Christ, today too we see you in the contrite, who in the depths of the misery of their sins, are able to cry out: Lord, remember me in your kingdom!

O Cross of Christ, today too we see you in the blessed and the saints who know how to cross the dark night of faith without ever losing trust in you and without claiming to understand your mysterious silence.

O Cross of Christ, today too we see you in families that live their vocation of married life in fidelity and fruitfulness.

O Cross of Christ, today too we see you in volunteers who generously assist those in need and the downtrodden.

O Cross of Christ, today too we see you in those persecuted for their faith who, amid their suffering, continue to offer an authentic witness to Jesus and the Gospel.

O Cross of Christ, today too we see you in those who dream, those with the heart of a child, who work to make the world a better place, ever more human and just.

In you, Holy Cross, we see God who loves even to the end, and we see the hatred of those who want to dominate, that hatred which blinds the minds and hearts of those who prefer darkness to light.

O Cross of Christ, Ark of Noah that saved humanity from the flood of sin, save us from evil and from the Evil One. O Throne of David and seal of the divine and eternal covenant, awaken us from the seduction of vanity! O cry of love, inspire in us a desire for God, for goodness and for light.

O Cross of Christ, teach us that the rising of the sun is more powerful than the darkness of night. O Cross of Christ, teach us that the apparent victory of evil vanishes before the empty tomb and before the certainty of the Resurrection and the love of God which nothing can defeat, obscure or weaken. Amen!

In 2015, Pope Francis turned to Retired Bishop Renato Corti of Novara, Italy. The bishop, a popular spiritual director and retreat leader (who directed St. John Paul II's 2005 Lenten retreat, which the dying pope followed via video link) penned his reflections imagining how Jesus experienced each of the Stations of the Cross.

Pope Francis's prayer on that occasion concluded with the recitation of the "Anima Christi" prayer, a medieval composition often attributed to St. Ignatius of Loyola, founder of the Jesuits. The pope's prayer reads:

O Christ Crucified and victorious, your Via Crucis is the consummation of your life; it is the icon of your obedience to the will of the Father; it is the realization of your infinite love for us sinners; it is the proof of your mission; it is the definitive fulfilment of revelation and

salvation history. The weight of your cross frees us of all our burdens.

In your obedience to the will of the Father, we understand our rebellion and disobedience. In you—sold, betrayed and crucified by your own people and loved ones—we see our daily betrayals and our habitual infidelities. In your innocence, Immaculate Lamb, we see our culpability. In your face—struck, spat on and disfigured—we see all the brutality of our sins. In the cruelty of your Passion, we see the cruelty of our hearts and of our actions. In your experience of being "abandoned," we see all those who have been abandoned by their relatives, by society, left without care and solidarity. In your body—stripped bare, pierced and lacerated—we see the bodies of our brothers and sisters left by the wayside, disfigured by our negligence and indifference. In your thirst, Lord, we see the thirst of your merciful Father who in you wanted to embrace, forgive and save all of humanity. In you, Divine Love, we see our brothers and sisters who are still being persecuted, decapitated and crucified for their faith in you, before our very eyes and often with our complicit silence.

Impress, Lord, in our hearts the sentiments of faith, hope, love and sorrow for our sins. Lead us to repent for our sins which crucified you. Lead us to transform our conversion made up of words into a conversion of life and deeds. Lead us to guard within us the living memory of your disfigured face, so as never to forget the terrible price you paid for our freedom. Jesus Crucified, strengthen faith in us so we do not fall in the face of temptation; revive hope in us so we do not go astray toward the seductions of the world; guard charity in us so we are not fooled by corruption and worldliness. Teach us that the cross is the way to the Resurrection. Teach us that Good Friday is the road to an Easter of light; teach us that God never forgets a single one of his children and never tires of forgiving us and of embracing us with his infinite mercy. Teach us, also, to never tire of asking for forgiveness, of believing in the boundless mercy of the Father.

"Soul of Christ, sanctify us. Body of Christ, save us. Blood of Christ, inebriate us. Water from the side of Christ, wash us. Passion of Christ, comfort us. O good Jesus, hear us. Within your wounds, hide us. Never let us be separated from you. From the malignant enemy, defend us. At the hour of death, call us; and bid us come to you. That with your saints we may praise you forever and ever." Amen.

To write the 2014 meditations, Pope Francis called upon Italian Archbishop Giancarlo Maria Bregantini of Campobasso-Boiano—a former factory worker, longtime prison chaplain, champion of the unemployed, and fiercely outspoken critic of the Italian mafia. Rather than composing his own prayer to conclude the Via Crucis, the pope made brief remarks, recited a prayer by 4th-century St. Gregory of Nazianzus, then added a few intentions. Here is what he said:

God placed on Jesus' cross all the weight of our sins, all the injustices perpetrated by every Cain against his brother, all the bitterness of the betrayal by Judas and by Peter, all the vanity of tyrants, all the arrogance of false friends. It was a heavy cross, like night experienced by abandoned people, heavy like the death of loved ones, heavy because it carries all the ugliness of evil. However, the cross is also glorious like the dawn after a long night, for it represents all the love of God, which is greater than our iniquities and our betrayals. In the cross we see the monstrosity of man, when he allows evil to guide him; but we also see the immensity of the mercy of God, who does not treat us according to our sins but according to his mercy.

Before the cross of Jesus, we apprehend in a way that we can almost touch with our hands how much we are eternally loved; before the cross we feel that we are "children" and not "things" or "objects," as St. Gregory of Nazianzus says, addressing Christ with this prayer: "Were it not for you, O my Christ, I would feel like a finite creature. I was born and I feel myself dissolve. I eat, I sleep, I rest and I walk, I fall ill and I recover. Longings and torments without number assail me, I enjoy the sun and how the earth bears fruit. Then, I die and my flesh turns to dust just like that of animals, who have not sinned. But what have I more than them? Nothing, if not God. Were it not for you, O Christ mine, I would feel myself a lost creature. O, our Jesus, guide us from the cross to the resurrection and teach us that evil shall not have the last word, but love, mercy and forgiveness. O Christ, help us to exclaim again: 'Yesterday I was crucified with Christ; today I am

glorified with Him. Yesterday I died with Him, today I
live with Him. Yesterday I was buried with Him, today I
am raised with Him.'"

Finally, all together, let us remember the sick, let us
remember all those who have been abandoned under
the weight of the cross, that they may find in the
trial of the cross the strength of hope, of hope, in the
resurrection and love of God.

The meditations for Pope Francis's first Via Crucis at the
Colosseum were commissioned by Pope Benedict XVI
before he announced his resignation in February 2013. The
new pope inherited the reflections composed by young
people in Lebanon in a project coordinated by Maronite
Patriarch Bechara Rai. Rather than offer his own prayer,
Pope Francis thanked those who prepared the service and
gave brief remarks that conveyed many of the thoughts he
would phrase as prayers in the years to come:

I do not wish to add too many words. One word should
suffice this evening, that is the Cross itself. The cross
is the word through which God has responded to evil
in the world. Sometimes it may seem as though God
does not react to evil, as if he is silent. And yet, God has
spoken, he has replied, and his answer is the cross of
Christ: a word which is love, mercy, forgiveness. It also
reveals a judgment, namely that God, in judging us,
loves us. Let us remember this: God judges us by loving
us. If I embrace his love then I am saved; if I refuse it,

then I am condemned, not by him, but my own self,
because God never condemns, he only loves and saves.

Dear brothers and sisters, the word of the cross is also
the answer which Christians offer in the face of evil,
the evil that continues to work in us and around us.
Christians must respond to evil with good, taking the
cross upon themselves as Jesus did. This evening we
have heard the witness given by our Lebanese brothers
and sisters: they composed these beautiful prayers and
meditations. We extend our heartfelt gratitude to them
for this work and for the witness they offer. We were able
to see this when Pope Benedict visited Lebanon: we saw
the beauty and the strong bond of communion joining
Christians together in that land and the friendship of
our Muslim brothers and sisters and so many others.
That occasion was a sign to the Middle East and to the
whole world: a sign of hope.

We now continue this Via Crucis in our daily lives. Let us
walk together along the Way of the Cross and let us do so
carrying in our hearts this word of love and forgiveness.
Let us go forward waiting for the Resurrection of Jesus,
who loves us so much. He is all love!

CHAPTER 3

PRAYERS TO MARY

Devotion to the Blessed Virgin Mary is a solid part of Catholic tradition and a mainstay in the spirituality and teaching of the popes. St. John Paul II's motto, *Totus Tuus* ("All yours"), and the large "M" on his coat of arms were just the most graphic elements of a devotion that led to a whole body of teaching about Mary, her role in Catholics' faith life and the importance of praying the rosary. Pope Francis's devotion is just as profound, as is seen in his teaching, his prayers and even his gestures. Whenever Pope Francis passes a statue or icon of Mary, he kisses it or allows his hand to rest tenderly upon it.

Pope Francis also brought to the attention of Catholics worldwide two Marian devotions dear to his heart, but which previously had a mainly local following: Mary, Undoer (or Untier) of Knots and Our Lady of Silence.

His devotion to Mary, Undoer of Knots began when he was a student in Germany and saw a painting of Mary in a local church; he promoted the devotion when he returned to Argentina, encouraging people to seek Mary's help in untying the knots of sin in their lives. During a Mass for the feast of Our Lady of Guadalupe in 2018, he said that Mary is "a woman who walks with the gentleness and tenderness of a mother, she makes her home in family life, she unties one knot after another of the many wrongs we manage to generate, and she teaches us to remain standing in the midst of storms."

Our Lady of Silence is a newer devotion, one that prizes and offers as a model the Gospel affirmation that "Mary kept all these things, reflecting on them in her heart" (Lk 2:19). The devotion also resonates with Pope Francis's frequent admonitions that people "bite their tongues" when tempted to gossip or speak ill of others.

Meeting with the Italian bishops in May 2013, he offered this prayer to "Mary, Mother of Silence":

**Mother of silence, who watches over the mystery of God,
Save us from the idolatry of the present time, to which
those who forget are condemned.
Purify the eyes of pastors with the eye-wash of memory:
Take us back to the freshness of the origins, for a
prayerful, penitent church.**

**Mother of the beauty that blossoms from faithfulness to
daily work,
Lift us from the torpor of laziness, pettiness and
defeatism.
Clothe pastors in the compassion that unifies, that
makes whole; let us discover the joy of a humble,
brotherly, serving church.**

**Mother of tenderness who envelops us in patience and
mercy,**

Help us burn away the sadness, impatience and rigidity
    of those who do not know what it means to belong.
Intercede with your Son to obtain that our hands, our
    feet, our hearts be agile: let us build the church with
    the truth of love.
Mother, we shall be the People of God, pilgrims bound
    for the kingdom. Amen.

A week after meeting the bishops, Pope Francis led a public recitation of the rosary to mark the end of the month of May, the month traditionally devoted to Mary. At the end of the rosary, he offered a related prayer to "Mary, woman of listening":

Mary, woman of listening, open our ears; grant us to know how to listen to the word of your Son Jesus among the thousands of words of this world; grant that we may listen to the reality in which we live, to every person we encounter, especially those who are poor, in need, in hardship.

Mary, woman of decision, illuminate our mind and our heart, so that we may obey, unhesitating, the word of your Son Jesus; give us the courage to decide, not to let ourselves be dragged along, letting others direct our life.

Mary, woman of action, obtain that our hands and feet move "with haste" toward others, to bring them the charity and love of your Son Jesus, to bring the light of the Gospel to the world, as you did.

Amen.

Also during that first year of his papacy, Pope Francis led a special prayer service in St. Peter's Square in the presence of the statue of Our Lady of Fatima, which was brought from the shrine in Portugal. At the end of the service, he offered a special prayer entrusting the world to the care of Mary:

Blessed Virgin Mary of Fatima,
with renewed gratitude for your motherly presence
we join in the voice of all generations that call
    you blessed.

We celebrate in you the great works of God,
who never tires of lowering himself in mercy over
    humanity,
afflicted by evil and wounded by sin,
to heal and to save it.

Accept with the benevolence of a Mother
this act of entrustment that we make in faith today,
before this your image, beloved to us.

We are certain that each one of us is precious in
    your eyes
and that nothing in our hearts has estranged you.

May that we allow your sweet gaze
to reach us and the perpetual warmth of your smile.

Guard our life with your embrace:
bless and strengthen every desire for good;
give new life and nourishment to faith;
sustain and enlighten hope;

awaken and animate charity;
guide us all on the path to holiness.

Teach us your own special love for the little and
    the poor,
for the excluded and the suffering,
for sinners and the wounded of heart:
gather all people under your protection
and give us all to your beloved Son, our Lord Jesus.

Amen.

Four years later in 2017, Pope Francis marked the 100th
anniversary of the Marian apparitions at Fatima by traveling
to the shrine. He composed a special prayer, using lines from
the traditional "Salve Regina" or "Hail, Holy Queen" and
expanding on them with more praise, reflections and petitions. The prayer included refrains by the faithful present:

Hail Holy Queen,
Blessed Virgin of Fatima,
Lady of Immaculate Heart,
our refuge and our way to God!

As a pilgrim of the light that comes to us from
    your hands,
I give thanks to God the Father, who in every time
    and place
is at work in human history;
As a pilgrim of the peace that, in this place, you
    proclaim,

I give praise to Christ, our peace, and I implore for
    the world
concord among all peoples;
As a pilgrim of the hope that the Spirit awakens,
I come as a prophet and messenger to wash the feet
    of all,
at the same table that unites us.

Refrain:

Ave O Clemens, Ave O pia!
Salve Regina Rosarii Fatimae.
Ave O clemens, Ave O pia!
Ave O dulcis Virgo Maria!

Hail, Mother of Mercy,
Lady robed in white!
In this place where, a hundred years ago
you made known to all the purposes of God's mercy,
I gaze at your robe of light
and, as a bishop robed in white,
I call to mind all those who,
robed in the splendor of their baptism,
desire to live in God
and tell the mysteries of Christ in order to obtain peace.

Refrain

Hail, life and sweetness,
Hail, our hope,
O Pilgrim Virgin, O Universal Queen!

In the depths of your being,
in your Immaculate Heart,
you keep the joys of men and women
as they journey to the heavenly homeland.
In the depths of your being,
in your Immaculate Heart,
you keep the sorrows of the human family,
as they mourn and weep in this valley of tears.
In the depths of your being,
in your Immaculate Heart,
adorn us with the radiance of the jewels of your crown
and make us pilgrims, even as you were a pilgrim.

With your virginal smile,
enliven the joy of Christ's church.
With your gaze of sweetness,
strengthen the hope of God's children.
With your hands lifted in prayer to the Lord,
draw all people together into one human family.

Refrain

O clement, O loving,
O sweet Virgin Mary,
Queen of the Rosary of Fatima!
Grant that we may follow the example of Blessed
    Francisco and Blessed Jacinta,
and of all who devote themselves to proclaiming
    the Gospel.
Thus, we will follow all paths
and everywhere make our pilgrim way;
we will tear down all walls

and cross every frontier,
as we go out to every periphery,
to make known God's justice and peace.

In the joy of the Gospel, we will be the church robed in
    white,
the whiteness washed in the blood of the Lamb,
blood that today too is shed in the wars tearing our
    world apart.
And so we will be, like you, an image of the column of
    light
that illumines the ways of the world,
making God known to all,
making known to all that God exists,
that God dwells in the midst of his people,
yesterday, today and for all eternity.

Refrain

Hail, Mother of the Lord,
Virgin Mary, Queen of the Rosary of Fatima!
Blessed among all women,
you are the image of the church robed in paschal light,
you are the honor of our people,
you are the victory over every assault of evil.

Prophecy of the merciful love of the Father,
Teacher of the message of Good News of the Son,
Sign of the burning fire of the Holy Spirit,
teach us, in this valley of joys and sorrows,
the eternal truths that the Father reveals to the little ones.

Show us the strength of your protective mantle.
In your Immaculate Heart,
be the refuge of sinners
and the way that leads to God.

In union with my brothers and sisters,
in faith, in hope and in love,
I entrust myself to you.
In union with my brothers and sisters, through you, I
    consecrate myself to God,
O Virgin of the Rosary of Fatima.

And at last, enveloped in the light that comes from your
    hands,
I will give glory to the Lord for ever and ever.
Amen.

Refrain

Honoring Mary by laying flowers at the foot of a statue in the center of Rome on the December 8 feast of the Immaculate Conception, previous popes would make a brief speech, but Pope Francis offers a prayer. The feast is a national holiday in Italy and while tourists come to see the pope at the Spanish Steps, it is a predominantly Roman celebration. The petitions Pope Francis raises to Mary usually include references to specific situations of need in the city and the nation.

At the 2019 celebration, he said:

O Mary Immaculate,
we gather around you once again.
The more we move forward in life

the more our gratitude to God increases for giving as a
    Mother to us who are sinners,
you, the Immaculate Conception.
Of all human beings, you are the only one preserved
    from sin, as Mother of Jesus,
the Lamb of God who takes away the sin of the world.
But this singular privilege of yours
was given to you for the good of us all, your children.
In fact, looking at you, we see the victory of Christ,
the victory of God's love over evil:
where sin abounded, namely, in the human heart,
grace has overflowed all the more,
through the gentle power of Jesus' Blood.

You, Mother, remind us that we are sinners, but we are
    no longer slaves to sin!
Through His Sacrifice, your Son
has broken the rule of evil and has overcome the world.
This tells all generations about your heart, clear as the
    sky where the wind has dissipated every cloud.
And so you remind us that being sinners and being
    corrupt is not the same thing: it is very different.
It is one thing to fall, but then, repenting, to get up again
    with the help of God's mercy.
Something else is hypocritical conspiracy with evil,
    corruption of the heart, that appears faultless on the
    outside,
but inside, is full of evil intentions and nasty selfishness.
Your crystal-clear purity calls us back to sincerity,
    transparency, simplicity.
How much we need to be liberated

from corruption of the heart, which is the greatest danger!
This seems impossible to us, we are so accustomed to it,
yet it is within easy reach. It is enough to look up at your
    Mother's smile, at your unspoiled beauty,
to feel once more that we are not meant for evil, but for
    good, for love, for God!

For this reason, O Virgin Mary,
today I entrust to you all those who, in this city
    and throughout the world, are burdened by
    disillusionment,
by discouragement because of sin;
those who think there is no longer hope for them,
that their sins are too many and too great,
and that God certainly does not have time to waste
    with them.
I entrust them to you, because not only are you a Mother
    and as such, you never stop loving your children,
but you are also Immaculate, full of grace,
and you can reflect into the darkest gloom a ray of the
    Risen Christ's light.
He, and He alone, breaks the chains of evil, frees from
    the most acute dependencies, unties from the most
    criminal bonds,
softens the hardest of hearts.
And if this happens within people,
how the face of the city changes!
In small gestures and big choices,
vicious circles gradually become virtuous, the quality of
    life improves
and the social climate becomes more breathable.

We thank you, Immaculate Mother,
for reminding us that, because of Jesus Christ's love,
we are no longer slaves to sin,
but free, free to love, to love one another,
to help one another as brothers and sisters, despite
    our differences—
and thank you for the differences between us.
Thank you, because with your purity, you encourage us
not to be ashamed of good, but of evil;
you help us to keep at a distance the evil one, who
    deceives us and draws us to himself, into coils of death;
you grant us the gentle reminder that we are children
    of God,
Father of immense goodness,
eternal source of life, beauty and love.
Amen.

His prayer in 2018 was:

Immaculate Mother,
on the day of your celebration, so dear to the
    Christian people,
I come to pay you homage in the heart of Rome.
In my soul I carry the faithful of this church
and all those who live in this city, especially the sick
    and those who due to various circumstances struggle
    harder to go on.

First and foremost we wish to thank you for the
    motherly care with which you accompany our
    journey:

how often we hear those who have experienced your
    intercession describe with teary eyes
the graces that you request for us from your Son Jesus!
I also think of an ordinary grace that you give to the
    people who live in Rome:
that of patiently facing the discomforts of daily life.
For this we ask you for the strength not to give in,
    but rather, to each do our part each day to improve
    things,
so that each one's care may make Rome more beautiful
    and livable for everyone;
so that each one's duty properly fulfilled may ensure the
    rights of everyone.
And thinking of the common good of this city,
we pray to you for those who play roles of great
    responsibility: may you obtain for them wisdom,
    foresight, the spirit of service and cooperation.

Blessed Virgin,
I wish to entrust to you in a particular way the priests of
    this diocese: pastors, assistant pastors, elderly priests
    who, with a shepherd's heart, continue to work at the
    service of the People of God,
the many student priests from every part of the world
    who cooperate in the parishes.
For all of them I ask you for the gentle joy of
    evangelizing and the gift of being fathers, close to the
    people, merciful.

To you, Lady wholly consecrated to God, I entrust
    the consecrated women in religious and in secular

life who, thank God, are more numerous in Rome
than in any other city in the world, and who form a
marvelous mosaic of nationalities and cultures.
For them I ask you for the joy to be, like you, spouses
and mothers, fruitful in prayer, in charity, in
compassion.

O Mother of Jesus,
I ask of you one last thing in this season of Advent,
reflecting on the days in which you and Joseph were in
distress for the then imminent birth of your child,
concerned because there was the census and you
too had to leave your town, Nazareth, and go to
Bethlehem. . . .
You know, Mother, what it means to carry life in your
womb and to feel indifference, rejection, at times
scorn around you.
For this reason I ask you to be close to families that
today in Rome, in Italy, in the entire world, are
experiencing similar situations, so that they not be
abandoned to themselves, but protected in their
rights, human rights which come before any other
justifiable need.

O Mary Immaculate,
dawn of hope at the horizon of humanity,
watch over this city,
over its houses, over its schools, over its offices, over
its shops,
over its factories, over its hospitals, over its prisons;

may no place lack the most valuable thing that Rome has, and which it preserves for the entire world, the testament of Jesus: "Love one another, as I have loved you" (cf. Jn 13:34).
Amen.

A year earlier, December 8, 2017, his prayer was:

Immaculate Mother,

For the fifth time I come to your feet as bishop of Rome,
to honor you on behalf of all the residents of this city.
We wish to thank you for the constant care
with which you accompany our journey,
the journey of families, of parishes, of religious communities;
the journey of those who each day, at times with difficulty,
pass through Rome to go to work;

of the sick, of the elderly, of all the poor,
of so many people who have immigrated here from lands of war and hunger.
Thank you because, as soon as we address a thought to you
or a gaze or a quick "Hail Mary,"
we always feel your maternal, tender and steadfast presence.

O Mother, help this city to develop "antibodies" against some of the viruses of our time:
indifference, which says: "It doesn't concern me";

the civic discourtesy which disregards the common
    good;
fear of those who are different or foreign;
transgression disguised as conformity;
the hypocrisy of accusing others while we do the
    same things;
resignation to environmental and ethical decay;
the exploitation of countless men and women.

Help us to reject these and other viruses with the
    antibodies that come from the Gospel.
Help us to develop the good habit of reading a passage
    from the Gospel each day
and, after your example, to cherish the Word in
    our hearts,
so that, as a good seed, it may bear fruit in our lives.

Immaculate Virgin,
175 years ago, not far from here, in the Church of
    Sant'Andrea delle Fratte, you touched the heart of
    Alphonse Ratisbonne, who at that moment
from an atheist and enemy of the church became
    Christian.
To him you revealed yourself as Mother of grace
    and mercy.

Grant that we, too, especially in trials and in temptation,
may fix our gaze on your open hands,
which let the Lord's grace come down to the earth,
and divest ourselves of any proud arrogance
so as to recognize ourselves as we truly are:
small and poor sinners, but always your children.

And thus to place our hand in yours

so as to be led back to Jesus, our brother and savior,
and to our heavenly Father, who never tires of waiting
for us
and of forgiving us when we return to Him.
Thank you, O Mother, for always listening to us!

May you bless the church that is in Rome,
bless this city and the entire world.
Amen.

The prayer he composed in 2016 read:

O Mary, our Immaculate Mother,
On your feast day I come to you,
And I come not alone:
I bring with me all those with whom your Son entrusted
to me,
In this city of Rome and in the entire world,
That you may bless them and preserve them from harm.

I bring to you, Mother, children,
Especially those who are alone, abandoned,
And for this reason are tricked and exploited.
I bring to you, Mother, families,
Who carry forward life and society
With their daily and hidden efforts;
In a special way the families who struggle the most
For their many internal and external problems.
I bring to you, Mother, all workers, both men and
women,

And I entrust to you especially those who, out of need,
Are forced to work in an unworthy profession
And those who have lost work or are unable to find it.

We are in need of your immaculate gaze,
To rediscover the ability to look upon persons and things
With respect and awareness,
Without egotistical or hypocritical interests.
We are in need of your immaculate heart,
To love freely,
Without secondary aims but seeking the good of the
    other,
With simplicity and sincerity, renouncing masks and
    tricks.
We are in need of your immaculate hands,
To caress with tenderness,
To touch the flesh of Jesus
In our poor, sick, or despised brethren,
To raise up those who have fallen and support those
    who waver.
We are in need of your immaculate feet,
To go toward those who know not how to make the first
    step,
To walk on the paths of those who are lost,
To find those who feel alone.

We thank you, O Mother, because in showing yourself
    to us
You free us of all stain of sin;
You remind us that what comes first is the grace of God,
The love of Jesus Christ who gave his life for us,

The strength of the Holy Spirit which renews all things.
Let us not give in to discouragement,
But, trusting in your constant help,
Let us engage ourselves fully in renewal of self,
Of this city and of the entire world.
Pray for us, Holy Mother of God!

His 2015 prayer was:

Virgin Mary,
on this day of celebration for your Immaculate
    Conception,
I come to give you the homage of the faith and love
of the holy people of God who live in this city and this
    diocese.

I come in the name of the families, with their joys and
    trials,
of children and young people, open to life,
of the elderly, rich in years and experience;
in particular, I come to you
on behalf of the sick, of prisoners,
of those who feel their journey is most difficult.
As pastor, I also come in the name
of those who arrived here from far-off lands in search of
    peace and of work.

Under your mantle there is a place for all
because you are the Mother of Mercy.
Your heart is full of tenderness for all of your children:
the tenderness of God, who took flesh in you

and became our brother, Jesus,
savior of every man and every woman.

Looking to you, our Immaculate Mother,
we recognize the victory of divine mercy
over sin and all its consequences;
and within us there is reignited a hope for a better life,
free from slavery, anger and fear.

Today, here, in the heart of Rome we hear your motherly
    voice
that calls us all to set off on a journey
toward that door, which is Christ.
You say to all: "Come, draw near with trust;
enter and receive the gift of mercy.
Do not be afraid, do not be ashamed:
The Father awaits you with open arms
to give you his forgiveness and welcome you into his home.
Come all to the source of peace and joy."

We thank you, Immaculate Mother,
because on this journey of reconciliation
you do not make us go alone, but accompany us;
you are close to us and support us in every difficulty.
Blessed are you, Mother, now and forever. Amen.

In 2014, again at the Spanish Steps in the heart of Rome, he
prayed:

Mary our Mother,

Today the People of God celebrate, they venerate you,
the Immaculate, ever preserved from the stain of sin.

Accept the homage I offer you in the name of the church in Rome and throughout the world.

Knowing that you, our Mother, are totally free from sin is a consolation to us.

Knowing that evil has no power over you fills us with hope and strength in our daily struggle against the threat of the evil one.

But in this struggle, we are not alone, we are not orphans, for Jesus, before dying on the Cross, gave you to us as our Mother.

Though we are sinners, we are still your children, the children of the Immaculate, called to that holiness that has shown resplendent in you by the grace of God from the beginning.

Inspired by this hope, today we invoke your motherly protection for us, our families, this city and the world.

Through your intercession, may the power of God's love that preserved you from original sin, free humanity from every form of spiritual and material slavery and make God's plan of salvation victorious in hearts and in history.

May grace prevail over pride in us, too, your children.

May we become merciful as our heavenly Father is merciful.

In this time leading up to the celebration of Jesus' birth, teach us to go against the current: to strip ourselves, to be humble and giving, to listen and be silent, to go out of ourselves, granting space to the beauty of God, the source of true joy.

Pray for us, our Immaculate Mother!

And presiding in 2013 over the act of veneration for the first time as pope and bishop of Rome, he prayed:

Virgin most holy and immaculate,
to you, the honor of our people,
and the loving protector of our city,
do we turn with loving trust.

You are all-beautiful, O Mary!
In you there is no sin.

Awaken in all of us a renewed desire for holiness:
May the splendor of truth shine forth in our words,
the song of charity resound in our works,
purity and chastity abide in our hearts and bodies,
and the full beauty of the Gospel be evident in our lives.

You are all-beautiful, O Mary!
In you the Word of God became flesh.

Help us always to heed the Lord's voice:
May we never be indifferent to the cry of the poor,
or untouched by the sufferings of the sick and those in
    need;

may we be sensitive to the loneliness of the elderly and
the vulnerability of children,
and always love and cherish the life of every
human being.

You are all-beautiful, O Mary!
In you is the fullness of joy born of life with God.

Help us never to forget the meaning of our earthly
journey:
May the kindly light of faith illumine our days,
the comforting power of hope direct our steps,
the contagious warmth of love stir our hearts;
and may our gaze be fixed on God, in whom true joy is
found.

You are all-beautiful, O Mary!
Hear our prayer, graciously hear our plea:
May the beauty of God's merciful love in Jesus abide in
our hearts,
and may this divine beauty save us, our city and the
entire world.

Amen.

CHAPTER 4

PRAYERS ABROAD

Pope Francis not only prays for people, he prays with them—serving as a public voice for the unspoken prayers that fill the hearts of the people he is with, especially when he travels. A striking example of that came in September 2019 when he visited a stone quarry in Madagascar. The people who work there and live on the edge of the quarry used to be garbage pickers, digging through trash to find anything they could resell or reuse. Now they break granite by hand and haul it away on their backs; the jobs do not pay well, but thanks to the organizational efforts of a missionary priest, members of the community earn enough to pool resources and feed and house their families. When the pope prayed in the dusty gray pit, he was as plain spoken as the men and women who work there, and he broadened their gaze to include struggling workers around the world, as well as the business owners who hire them:

God our Father, creator of heaven and earth,
we thank you for gathering us as brothers and sisters in
     this place.

Before this rock, split by human labor,
we pray to you for workers everywhere.

We pray for those who work with their hands
and with immense physical effort:
Soothe their wearied frames,
that they may tenderly caress their children
and join in their games.
Grant them unfailing spiritual strength and
    physical health,
lest they succumb beneath the burden of their labors.

Grant that the fruits of their work
may ensure a dignified life to their families.
May they come home at night to warmth, comfort
    and encouragement
and together, under your gaze,
find true joy.

May our families know that the joy of earning our
    daily bread
becomes perfect when that bread is shared.
May our children not be forced to work,
but receive schooling and continue their studies,
and may their teachers devote themselves fully to their task,
without needing other work to make a decent living.

God of justice, touch the hearts of owners
    and managers.
May they make every effort
to ensure that workers receive a just wage
and enjoy conditions respectful of their human dignity.

Father, in your mercy, take pity on those who lack work.
May unemployment—the cause of such great misery—
disappear from our societies.
May all know the joy and dignity of earning their
daily bread,
and bringing it home to support their loved ones.

Create among workers a spirit of authentic solidarity.
May they learn to be attentive to one another,
To encourage one another, to support those in difficulty
and to lift up those who have fallen.

Let their hearts not yield to hatred, resentment
or bitterness in the face of injustice.
May they keep alive their hope for a better world, and
work to that end.

Together, may they constructively
defend their rights.
Grant that their voices and demands may be heard.

God our Father, you have made St. Joseph,
foster father of Jesus and courageous spouse of the
Virgin Mary,
protector of workers throughout the world.
To him I entrust all those who labor here, at Akamasoa,
and all the workers of Madagascar,
especially those experiencing uncertainty and hardship.
May he keep them in the love of your Son
and sustain them in their livelihood and in their hope.

Amen.

Earlier in 2019, Pope Francis had gone to Skopje, North Macedonia, the birthplace of St. Teresa of Kolkata. With dozens of Missionaries of Charity and many of the poor they care for, the pope prayed that all people would be inspired by her selfless love and would work for justice. The prayer he recited on the site of the church where St. Teresa was baptized in 1910 was:

God, father of mercy and all goodness, we thank you for giving us the life and the charism of St. Mother Teresa. In your boundless providence, you called her to bear witness to your love among the poorest of the poor in India and throughout the world. She was able to do much good to those in greatest need, for she saw in every man and woman the face of your Son. Docile to your Spirit, she became the prayerful cry of the poor and of all those who hunger and thirst for justice. Taking up the words uttered by Jesus on the cross: "I thirst" (Jn 19:28), Mother Teresa sated the thirst of the crucified Lord by accomplishing works of merciful love.

St. Mother Teresa, mother of the poor, we ask for your special intercession and help, here in this city where you were born, where you had your home. Here you received the gift of rebirth in the sacraments of Christian initiation. Here you heard the first words of faith in your family and in the community of the faithful. Here you began to see and meet people in need, the poor and the helpless. Here you learned from your parents to love those in greatest need and to help them. Here, in

the silence of the church, you heard the call of Jesus to follow him as a religious in the missions.

Here in this place, we ask you to intercede with Jesus, that we too may obtain the grace to be watchful and attentive to the cry of the poor, those deprived of their rights, the sick, the outcast and the least of our brothers and sisters. May he grant us the grace to see him in the eyes of all who look to us in their need. May he grant us a heart capable of loving God present in every man and woman, a heart capable of recognizing him in those who experience suffering and injustice. May he grant us the grace to become signs of love and hope in our own day, when so many are poor, abandoned, marginalized and migrants. May he grant that our love not only be on our lips, but that it be effective and genuine, so that we may bear credible witness to the church whose duty it is to proclaim the Good News to the poor, freedom to prisoners, joy to the afflicted and the grace of salvation to all.

St. Mother Teresa, pray for this city, for this people, for its church and for all those who wish to follow Christ, the Good Shepherd, as his disciples, by carrying out works of justice, love, mercy, peace and service. To follow him, who came not to be served but to serve, and to give his life for many: Christ our Lord. Amen.

While Pope Francis will improvise brief petitions to God, the prayers that are formally set in the schedule of his papal trips—especially during Masses and other liturgies—are written well in advance and published as a book. That was not the case, however, when he went to Dublin, Ireland, in August 2018 and came face-to-face with the suffering of survivors of clerical sexual abuse and a Catholic community reeling from the scandal. At a large Mass in the city's Phoenix Park, the pope told the gathered crowd, "Yesterday I met with eight persons who are survivors of the abuse of power, the abuse of conscience and sexual abuse. In reflecting on what they told me, I wish to implore the Lord's mercy for these crimes and to ask forgiveness for them."

He then prayed:

We ask forgiveness for the cases of abuse in Ireland, the abuse of power, the abuse of conscience and sexual abuse on the part of representatives of the church. In a special way, we ask forgiveness for all those abuses that took place in different kinds of institutions directed by men and women religious and other members of the church. We also ask forgiveness for cases in which many minors were exploited for their labor.

We ask forgiveness for all those times when, as a church, we did not offer to the survivors of any type of abuse compassion and the pursuit of justice and truth by concrete actions. We ask forgiveness.

We ask forgiveness for some members of the hierarchy who took no responsibility for these painful situations and kept silent. We ask forgiveness.

We ask forgiveness those children who were taken away from their mothers and for all those times when so

many single mothers who tried to find their children
that had been taken away, or those children who tried to
find their mothers, were told that this was a mortal sin.
It is not a mortal sin; it is the Fourth Commandment!
We ask forgiveness.

May the Lord preserve and increase this sense of shame
and repentance, and grant us the strength to ensure that
it never happens again and that justice is done. Amen.

Visiting Lithuania in 2018, Pope Francis toured the former
headquarters of the Soviet KGB in Vilnius, the country's
capital. The communist authorities tortured thousands of
people in the building and more than 1,000 were executed
there in the 1940s. Joined by retired Archbishop Sigitas
Tamkevicius of Kaunas, who had been imprisoned for
"anti-Soviet propaganda" in the 1980s, Pope Francis prayed:

"My God, my God, why have you forsaken me?"
(Mt 27:46)

Your cry, Lord, continues to resound. It echoes within
these walls that recall of the sufferings endured by so
many sons and daughters of this people. Lithuanians
and those from other nations paid in their own flesh
the price of the thirst for absolute power on the part of
those who sought complete domination.

Your cry, O Lord, is echoed in the cry of the innocent
who, in union with you, cry out to heaven. It is the Good
Friday of sorrow and bitterness, of abandonment and
powerlessness, of cruelty and meaninglessness that

this Lithuanian people experienced as a result of the unrestrained ambition that hardens and blinds the heart.

In this place of remembrance, Lord, we pray that your cry may keep us alert. That your cry, Lord, may free us from the spiritual sickness that remains a constant temptation for us as a people: forgetfulness of the experiences and sufferings of those who have gone before us.

In your cry, and in the lives of all who suffered so greatly in the past, may we find the courage to commit ourselves decisively to the present and to the future. May that cry encourage us to not succumb to the fashions of the day, to simplistic slogans or to efforts to diminish or take away from any person the dignity you have given them.

Lord, may Lithuania be a beacon of hope. May it be a land of memory and action, constantly committed to fighting all forms of injustice. May it promote creative efforts to defend the rights of all persons, especially those most defenseless and vulnerable. And may Lithuania be for all a teacher in the way to reconcile and harmonize diversity.

Lord, grant that we may not be deaf to the plea of all those who cry out to heaven in our own day.

Visiting Colombia in 2017, Pope Francis praised efforts to end the civil strife there and presided over a prayer service where victims and perpetrators of violence took symbolic steps toward reconciliation. The event took place under the crucifix known as the "Black Christ of Bojaya," an image of Jesus whose arms and legs were blown off in 2002 when an improvised homemade mortar launched by rebels crashed through the roof of a church and exploded, killing at least 74 people who were hiding there. The pope prayed:

O black Christ of Bojayá,
who remind us of your passion and death;
together with your arms and feet
they have torn away your children
who sought refuge in you.

O black Christ of Bojayá,
who look tenderly upon us
and in whose face is serenity;
your heart beats
so that we may be received in your love.

O black Christ of Bojayá,
Grant us to commit ourselves to restoring your body.
May we be your feet that go forth to encounter
our brothers and sisters in need;
your arms to embrace
those who have lost their dignity;
your hands to bless and console
those who weep alone.

Make us witnesses
to your love and infinite mercy.

Amen.

At another scene of inexplicable deaths and suffering—Ground Zero in New York—Pope Francis gathered with representatives of many religions in 2015. He prayed:

O God of love, compassion and healing,
look on us, people of many different faiths
and religious traditions,
who gather today on this hallowed ground,
the scene of unspeakable violence and pain.

We ask you in your goodness
to give eternal light and peace
to all who died here:
the heroic first-responders:
our firefighters, police officers,
emergency service workers
and Port Authority personnel,
along with all the innocent men and women
who were victims of this tragedy
simply because their work or service
brought them here on September 11.

We ask you, in your compassion,
to bring healing to those who,
because of their presence here fourteen years ago,
continue to suffer from injuries and illness.

Heal, too, the pain of still-grieving families
and all who lost loved ones in this tragedy.
Give them strength to continue their lives
with courage and hope.

We are mindful as well
of those who suffered death, injury and loss
on the same day at the Pentagon
and in Shanksville, Pennsylvania.
Our hearts are one with theirs
as our prayer embraces their pain and suffering.

God of peace, bring your peace to our violent world:
peace in the hearts of all men and women
and peace among the nations of the earth.
Turn to your way of love
those whose hearts and minds
are consumed with hatred,
and who justify killing in the name of religion.

God of understanding,
overwhelmed by the magnitude of this tragedy,
we seek your light and guidance
as we confront such terrible events.

Grant that those whose lives were spared
may live so that the lives lost here
may not have been lost in vain.

Comfort and console us, strengthen us in hope,
and give us the wisdom and courage
to work tirelessly for a world
where true peace and love reign
among nations and in the hearts of all.

On other visits, like the one to Mother Teresa's hometown,
Pope Francis taps into pride in local heroes or longstanding

local devotions to pray that local Catholics today would learn to live the Christian virtues more fully and become truly missionary disciples.

Before the relics of Peruvian martyrs in Lima in 2018, he prayed:

God our Father,
through Jesus Christ
you founded your church
on the rock of the Apostles,
that, guided by the Holy Spirit,
she may be a sign and instrument
of your love and mercy in the world:
we thank you for the gifts you have
bestowed upon our church in Lima.

We thank you in a special way
for the holiness that has flourished in our land.
Our archdiocesan church has been made fruitful
by the apostolic labors of St. Turibius of Mogrovejo,
enlarged by the prayer, penance and charity
of St. Rose of Lima and St. Martin de Porres,
adorned by the missionary zeal of St. Francisco Solano
and the humble service of St. Juan Macías.
It has been blessed by the witness of Christian life and
**   fidelity to the Gospel**
of many others of our brothers and sisters.
We give you thanks for all that you have accomplished in
**   our history**
and we ask you to keep us faithful to the heritage we
**   have received.**

Help us to be a church that goes forth,
drawing near to all, especially the less fortunate.
Teach us to be missionary disciples
of Jesus Christ, the Lord of Miracles,
living in love, seeking unity
and practicing mercy,
so that, protected by the intercession
of Our Lady of Evangelization,
we may live the joy of the Gospel
and proclaim it before the world.

And, visiting Cuba in 2015 where devotion endures to Our Lady of Charity, also known as Our Lady of El Cobre, the pope prayed:

Our Lady of Charity of El Cobre,
Patroness of Cuba!
Hail, Mary,
full of grace!
You are the beloved daughter of the Father,
Mother of Christ, our God,
the living temple
of the Holy Spirit.

You carry in your name,
Virgin of Charity,
the memory of God who is love,
the memory of the new commandments of Jesus,
the evocation of the Holy Spirit:
love poured into our hearts,
the fire of charity

sent on Pentecost
upon the church,
the gift of the full freedom
of the children of God.

Blessed are you among women
and blessed is the fruit
of your womb, Jesus!
You came to visit our people
And you chose to remain with us
As Mother and Lady of Cuba,
on our pilgrimage
through the paths of history.

Your name and your image
are carved
into the hearts and minds
of all Cubans,
both in the country and abroad,
as a sign of hope
and the center of brotherly communion.
Holy Mary, Mother of God
and our Mother!

Pray for us
before your Son Jesus Christ,
intercede for us
with your motherly heart,
flooded with the love of the Holy Spirit.
Increase our faith,
awaken our hope,
broaden and strengthen our love.

Watch over our families,
protect our young people and our children,
console those who suffer.
Be the mother of the faithful
and of the pastors of the church,
model and star of the new evangelization.

Mother of reconciliation!
Gather your people
scattered around the earth.
Make of our Cuban nation
a house of brothers and sisters
that this people may open wide
her mind, her heart
and her life to Christ,
the one Savior and Redeemer,
who lives and reigns with the Father
and the Holy Spirit
forever and ever.

Amen.

People who know Pope Francis's biography know how important he considers the Latin American bishops' meeting in Aparecida, Brazil, in 2007. Then-Cardinal Jorge Mario Bergoglio of Buenos Aires was elected to head the committee drafting the conference's final document—a massive text on evangelization that covers everything from parish outreach to care for the environment. In his papacy, Pope Francis has echoed and amplified many of the document's affirmations. But he also has spoken about the experience of the bishops' meeting at the Marian shrine in Aparecida in a hall under the church as pilgrims prayed above. Returning to the shrine as pope in 2013, he made a very personal "Act of Consecration to Our Lady of Aparecida":

Mary Most Holy by the merits of our Lord Jesus Christ, in your beloved image of Aparecida, spread infinite favors over all Brazil.

I, unworthy to be counted among your sons and daughters but full of desire to share in the blessings of your mercy, lie prostrate at your feet. To you I consecrate my intentions, that they may ever dwell on the love that you merit; to you I consecrate my tongue that it may ever praise you and spread your devotion; to you I consecrate my heart, that, after God, I may love you above all things.

Receive me, incomparable Queen, you whom Christ Crucified gave to us as Mother, and count me among your blessed sons and daughters; take me under your protection; come to my aid in all my needs, both spiritual and temporal, and above all at the hour of my death.

Bless me, heavenly helper, and through your powerful intercession, give me strength in my weakness, so that, by serving you faithfully in this life, I may praise you, love you and give you thanks in heaven, for all eternity. May it be so!

CHAPTER 5

PRAYERS AFTER PREACHING

Pope Francis often ends his homilies with a call to prayer; he will preach on what the day's Mass readings call Christians to, and he will conclude by urging the congregation to ask God to make that happen. That is precisely what he did in Philadelphia in 2015 at the end of his homily at a Mass closing the World Meeting of Families. He prayed: **"May God grant that all of us may be prophets of the joy of the Gospel, the Gospel of the family and family love, as disciples of the Lord. May he grant us the grace to be worthy of that purity of heart which is not scandalized by the Gospel! Amen."**

Because the pope wants his weekday Masses in the chapel of his residence to be intimate experiences of prayer and not public events, the Vatican has never published a complete collection of the morning homilies although coverage of them in the Vatican newspaper and Vatican News has increased over time. That changed at the height of the 2020 coronavirus pandemic when Pope Francis's early morning Masses were livestreamed. He offered each Mass for a special intention: for medical workers, for the sick, for those dying alone, for parents, for the unemployed and for supermarket workers, sanitation workers, and others whose jobs were deemed "essential," placing them at risk of contagion. (The Vatican made the pope's COVID-19 prayers and homilies available as a book, *Strong in the Face of Tribulation*.)

A full record is available on the Vatican website of Pope Francis's homilies at public Masses, whether celebrated with tens of thousands of people in St. Peter's Square or barely more than 100 people at a parish on the outskirts of Rome. He celebrated his first Mass as pope March 14, 2013, the morning after his election. The liturgy was in the Sistine Chapel, where he was elected, and the cardinals who chose him to succeed retired Pope Benedict XVI were the concelebrants. His brief homily focused on setting out in faith, building up the church and explicitly professing faith in Jesus Christ. He ended the homily saying:

**My wish is that all of us, after these days of grace,
will have the courage, yes, the courage, to walk in the
presence of the Lord, with the Lord's Cross; to build the
church on the Lord's blood which was poured out on
the Cross; and to profess the one glory: Christ crucified.
And in this way, the church will go forward.**

**My prayer for all of us is that the Holy Spirit, through
the intercession of the Blessed Virgin Mary, our Mother,
will grant us this grace: to walk, to build, to profess Jesus
Christ crucified. Amen.**

Pope Francis gave an even shorter homily a few days later when he celebrated Mass in the little Vatican parish church of St. Anna. And his prayer suggestion at the end the homily about God's overwhelming mercy was brief as well: "**The Lord never tires of forgiving: never! It is we who tire of asking his forgiveness. Let us ask for the grace not to tire of asking forgiveness, because he never tires of forgiving. Let us ask for this grace."**

Elected March 13, 2013, he formally began his ministry with a liturgy on the March 19 feast of St. Joseph to whom he has a strong and continuing devotion. He ended that homily saying, "**I implore the intercession of the Virgin Mary, St. Joseph, Sts. Peter and Paul, and St. Francis, that the Holy Spirit may accompany my ministry, and I ask all of you to pray for me! Amen."**

Celebrating his first chrism Mass as bishop of Rome March 28, 2013, he prayed with priests:

May God the Father renew in us the Spirit of holiness with whom we have been anointed. May he renew his Spirit in our hearts, that this anointing may spread to everyone, even to those 'outskirts' where our faithful people most look for it and most appreciate it. May our people sense that we are the Lord's disciples; may they feel that their names are written upon our priestly vestments and that we seek no other identity; and may they receive through our words and deeds the oil of gladness which Jesus, the Anointed One, came to bring us. Amen.

The pope's prayer suggestion often follows a question or a prompt for an examination of conscience, one that he addresses to himself as well as to his congregation. For example, on the feast of the Body and Blood of the Lord in 2013, he ended the homily by saying:

Let us ask ourselves this evening, in adoring Christ who is really present in the Eucharist: do I let myself be transformed by him? Do I let the Lord who gives himself to me guide me to going out ever more from my little enclosure in order to give, to share, to love him and others?

Brothers and sisters: following, communion, sharing. Let us pray that participation in the Eucharist may always be an incentive to follow the Lord every day, to be instruments of communion and to share what we are with him and with our neighbor. Our life will then be truly fruitful. Amen.

A few years later in 2018, he ended his Corpus Christi homily with the prayer:

Come, Lord, and visit us.
We welcome you into our hearts,
our families and our city.
We thank you because you have prepared for us
the food of life and a place in your Kingdom.
Make us active in preparing your way,
joyous in bringing you, who are life, to others,
and thus to bring fraternity, justice and peace
to our streets. Amen.

The pope also led an examination of conscience on his first visit outside of Rome as pope; he went in July 2013 to

Lampedusa, the southern Italian island that is the first landing place of many migrants and refugees attempting to cross the Mediterranean from northern Africa. Each year hundreds drown in their search for safety and a better life. At Mass on the island, Pope Francis ended his homily:

Let us ask the Lord to remove the part of Herod that lurks in our hearts; let us ask the Lord for the grace to weep over our indifference, to weep over the cruelty of our world, of our own hearts, and of all those who in anonymity make social and economic decisions which open the door to tragic situations like this. "Has any one wept?" Today has anyone wept in our world?

Lord, in this liturgy, a penitential liturgy, we beg forgiveness for our indifference to so many of our brothers and sisters. Father, we ask your pardon for those who are complacent and closed amid comforts which have deadened their hearts; we beg your forgiveness for those who by their decisions on the global level have created situations that lead to these tragedies. Forgive us, Lord!

At times, Pope Francis also invites the congregation to follow a practice he learned from St. Ignatius of Loyola, founder of the Jesuit order to which the pope belonged. The practice is a form of prayer that begins by imagining oneself in a biblical scene, perhaps as one of the characters. Visiting a Rome parish in January 2014, he ended his homily:

I invite you to do something: let us close our eyes, let us imagine the scene on the banks of the river, John as

he is baptizing and Jesus who is approaching. And let us listen to John's voice: "Behold, the Lamb of God, who takes away the sin of the world." Let us watch Jesus and in silence, each one of us, say something to Jesus from his heart. In silence.

And, after pausing for that silent, imaginative reflection, he prayed:

May the Lord Jesus, who is meek, who is good—he is a lamb—who came to take away sin, accompany us on the path of our life.

Pope Francis's entire homily on Palm Sunday 2014 was a guided lesson in that imaginative prayer process. It was brief, but filled with questions for reflection:

This week begins with the festive procession with olive branches: the entire populace welcomes Jesus. The children and young people sing, praising Jesus.

But this week continues in the mystery of Jesus' death and his resurrection. We have just listened to the Passion of our Lord. We might well ask ourselves just one question: Who am I? Who am I before my Lord? Who am I before Jesus who enters Jerusalem amid the enthusiasm of the crowd? Am I ready to express my joy, to praise him? Or do I stand back? Who am I, before the suffering Jesus?

We have just heard many, many names. The group of leaders, some priests, the Pharisees, the teachers of the law, who had decided to kill Jesus. They were waiting for the chance to arrest him. Am I like one of them?

We have also heard another name: Judas. Thirty pieces of silver. Am I like Judas? We have heard other names too: the disciples who understand nothing, who fell asleep while the Lord was suffering. Has my life fallen asleep? Or am I like the disciples, who did not realize what it was to betray Jesus? Or like that other disciple, who wanted to settle everything with a sword? Am I like them? Am I like Judas, who feigns loved and then kisses the Master in order to hand him over, to betray him? Am I a traitor? Am I like those people in power who hastily summon a tribunal and seek false witnesses: am I like them? And when I do these things, if I do them, do I think that in this way I am saving the people?

Am I like Pilate? When I see that the situation is difficult, do I wash my hands and dodge my responsibility, allowing people to be condemned— or condemning them myself?

Am I like that crowd which was not sure whether they were at a religious meeting, a trial or a circus, and then chose Barabbas? For them it was all the same: it was more entertaining to humiliate Jesus.

Am I like the soldiers who strike the Lord, spit on him, insult him, who find entertainment in humiliating him?

Am I like the Cyrenean, who was returning from work, weary, yet was good enough to help the Lord carry his cross?

Am I like those who walked by the cross and mocked Jesus: "He was so courageous! Let him come down from the cross and then we will believe in him!" Mocking Jesus . . .

Am I like those fearless women, and like the mother of Jesus, who were there, and who suffered in silence?

Am I like Joseph, the hidden disciple, who lovingly carries the body of Jesus to give it burial?

Am I like the two Marys, who remained at the tomb, weeping and praying?

Am I like those leaders who went the next day to Pilate and said, "Look, this man said that he was going to rise again. We cannot let another fraud take place!" and who block life, who block the tomb, in order to maintain doctrine, lest life come forth?

Where is my heart? Which of these persons am I like? May this question remain with us throughout the entire week.

On Christmas, Pope Francis has placed himself before the Baby Jesus when composing his short prayer at the end of a homily. For example, in 2017 he ended his midnight Mass homily with:

Moved by the joy of the gift, little Child of Bethlehem, we ask that your crying may shake us from our indifference and open our eyes to those who are suffering. May your tenderness awaken our sensitivity and make us recognize our call to see you in all those who arrive in our cities, in our histories, in our lives. May your revolutionary tenderness persuade us to feel our call to be agents of the hope and tenderness of our people.

And the next year, he put himself among the shepherds calling each other to go to Bethlehem to see the newborn king:

I want to come to Bethlehem, Lord, because there you await me. I want to realize that you, lying in a manger, are the bread of my life. I need the tender fragrance of your love so that I, in turn, can be bread broken for the world. Take me upon your shoulders, Good Shepherd; loved by you, I will be able to love my brothers and sisters and to take them by the hand. Then it will be Christmas, when I can say to you: "Lord you know everything; you know that I love you" (cf. Jn 21:17).

He leads public prayers for Christian unity each January, presiding over an ecumenical celebration of evening prayer at the end of the Week of Prayer for Christian Unity. There, too, he usually suggests a prayer for the entire congregation, as he did in 2014:

Dear brothers and sisters, let us ask the Lord Jesus, who has made us living members of his body, to keep us deeply united to him, to help us overcome our conflicts, our divisions and our self-seeking; and let us remember that unity is always better than conflict! And so, may he help us to be united to one another by one force—the

power of love which the Holy Spirit pours into our hearts (cf. Rom 5:5). Amen.

Several months later, celebrating Mass in Amman, Jordan, where a Christian minority lives and works with a Muslim majority, Pope Francis ended his homily praying for unity there, as well:

Let us ask the Spirit to prepare our hearts to encounter our brothers and sisters, so that we may overcome our differences rooted in political thinking, language, culture and religion. Let us ask him to anoint our whole being with the oil of his mercy, which heals the injuries caused by mistakes, misunderstandings and disputes. And let us ask him for the grace to send us forth, in humility and meekness, along the demanding but enriching path of seeking peace.

Presiding in 2017 over a prayer service for peace in Congo and South Sudan, Pope Francis turned most of his homily into a prayer:

Without you, Lord, our prayer would be in vain, and our hope for peace an illusion. But you are alive. You are at work for us and with us. You are our peace!

May the risen Lord break down the walls of hostility that today divide brothers and sisters, especially in South Sudan and the Democratic Republic of Congo.

May he comfort those women who are the victims of violence in war zones and throughout the world.

May he protect children who suffer from conflicts in which they have no part, but which rob them of their childhood and at times of life itself. How hypocritical it is to deny the mass murder of women and children! Here war shows its most horrid face.

May the Lord help all the little ones and the poor of our world to continue to believe and trust that the kingdom of God is at hand, in our midst, and is "justice, peace and joy in the Holy Spirit" (Rom 14:17). May he sustain all those who day by day strive to combat evil with good, and with words and deeds of fraternity, respect, encounter and solidarity.

May the Lord strengthen in government officials and all leaders a spirit which is noble, upright, steadfast and courageous in seeking peace through dialogue and negotiation.

May the Lord enable all of us to be peacemakers wherever we find ourselves, in our families, in school, at work, in the community, in every setting. "Let us wash the feet" of one another, in imitation of our Master and Lord. To him be glory and praise, now and forever. Amen.

Sometimes his homilies lead Pope Francis to pray for specific groups of people, like he did when preaching at the chrism Mass in 2014:

I ask the Lord Jesus to make better known the joy of elderly priests, whether healthy or infirm. It is the joy of the Cross, which springs from the knowledge that we possess an imperishable treasure in perishable earthen vessels. May these priests find happiness wherever they are; may they experience already, in the passage of the years, a taste of eternity. May they know, Lord, the joy of handing on the torch, the joy of seeing new generations of their spiritual children, and of hailing the promises from afar, smiling and at peace, in that hope which does not disappoint.

Marking the feasts of All Souls and All Saints, Pope Francis usually celebrates an evening Mass each Nov. 1 in a different cemetery, gathered with people whose loved ones are buried there. In 2014, at Rome's Verano cemetery, he preached about living with the hope of coming face-to-face with God at the end of one's life. And he prayed:

May the Lord help us and give us the grace of this hope, but also the grace of courage to emerge from all this destruction, devastation, the relativism of life, the exclusion of others, exclusion of values, exclusion of all that the Lord has given us: the exclusion of peace. May he deliver us from this and give us the grace to walk in the hope of finding ourselves one day face-to-face with Him. And this hope, brothers and sisters, does not disappoint!

Likewise, celebrating the feast of Pentecost, he always ends with the prayer, "Come, Holy Spirit," but often, like in 2019, he expands that prayer:

Holy Spirit, harmony of God, you who turn fear into trust and self-centeredness into self-gift, come to us. Grant us the joy of the resurrection and perennially young hearts. Holy Spirit, our harmony, you who make of us one body, pour forth your peace upon the church and our world. Holy Spirit, make us builders of concord, sowers of goodness, apostles of hope.

Celebrating Pentecost in 2020, in the midst of the coronavirus pandemic, he prayed:

Holy Spirit, memory of God, revive in us the memory of the gift received. Free us from the paralysis of selfishness and awaken in us the desire to serve, to do good. Even worse than this crisis is the tragedy of squandering it by closing in on ourselves. Come, Holy Spirit: you are harmony; make us builders of unity. You always give yourself; grant us the courage to go out of ourselves, to love and help each other, in order to become one family. Amen.

Sometimes the prayer at the end of Pope Francis's homily is what Italians call a *fervorino*, basically a short exhortation. For example, preaching in Tibilisi, Georgia, in 2016, Pope Francis spoke about St. Therese of Lisieux and her focus on cultivating complete, child-like trust and faith in God. The pope ended the homily saying, **"Together let us all implore today the grace of a simple heart, of a heart that believes and lives in the gentle strength of love; let us ask to live in peaceful and complete trust in God's mercy."**

Creating five new cardinals in 2017, he ended his homily with the prayer: **"Let us ask the Holy Spirit to bridge every gap between our hearts and the heart of Christ, so that our lives may be completely at the service of God and all our brothers and sisters."** Similarly, when celebrating a Mass with catechists in 2016, he ended with the prayer: **"May the Lord give us the grace to be renewed every day by the joy of the first proclamation to us: Jesus died and is risen, Jesus loves us personally! May he give us the strength to live and proclaim the commandment of love, overcoming the blindness of appearances, and worldly sadness. May he make us sensitive to the poor, who are not an afterthought in the Gospel but an important page, always open before all."**

Learning to love the poor like Jesus did is a frequent subject of Pope Francis's preaching and of his prayer. It is an important part of what he calls being a "missionary disciple," one who shares the Good News of God's love through both word and action. Pope Francis established the World Day of the Poor to focus Catholics' attention on their obligations to their needy brothers and sisters and to highlight how they, too, belong to the church. At Mass for the celebration in 2018, he ended his homily with the simple prayer: **"Stretch out your hand to us, Lord, and take hold of us. Help us to love as you love. Teach us to leave behind all that is passing, to be a source of reassurance to those around us, and to give freely to all those in need. Amen."**

But he also often remembers in prayer those who have been persecuted and even put to death for living their faith. In

CHAPTER 6

PRAYERS FOR
SPECIAL OCCASIONS

Pope Francis's vision of his responsibility to pray with and for his flock and to help them to pray means that he composes special prayers for special occasions and special needs. And, at least in the first seven years of his pontificate, nothing was more special that the proclamation of God's merciful love for all people. Proclaiming a Jubilee Year of Mercy, celebrated from December 8, 2015, to November 20, 2016, the pope wrote a special prayer:

Lord Jesus Christ,
you have taught us to be merciful like the heavenly
   Father,
and have told us that whoever sees you sees him.
Show us your face and we will be saved.
Your loving gaze freed Zacchaeus and Matthew from
   being enslaved by money;
the adulteress and Magdalene from seeking happiness
   only in created things;
made Peter weep after his betrayal,

and assured paradise to the repentant thief.

Let us hear, as if addressed to each one of us, the words
that you spoke to the Samaritan woman:

"If you knew the gift of God!"

You are the visible face of the invisible Father,

of the God who manifests his power above all by
forgiveness and mercy:

let the church be your visible face in the world, its Lord
risen and glorified.

You willed that your ministers would also be clothed in
weakness

in order that they may feel compassion for those in
ignorance and error:

let everyone who approaches them feel sought after,
loved and forgiven by God.

Send your Spirit and consecrate every one of us with its
anointing,

so that the Jubilee of Mercy may be a year of grace from
the Lord,

and your church, with renewed enthusiasm, may bring
good news to the poor,

proclaim liberty to captives and the oppressed,

and restore sight to the blind.

We ask this of you, Lord Jesus, through the intercession
of Mary, Mother of Mercy; you who live and reign
with the Father and the Holy Spirit for ever and ever.

Amen.

And before the extraordinary session of the Synod of Bishops on the family met in 2014, he composed a prayer that he asked all Catholics to recite, and the prayer also was included in the working document for the 2015 sessions of the ordinary synod, which continued the discussions on ministry to families and the modern challenges families face:

Jesus, Mary and Joseph,
in you we contemplate
the splendor of true love,
to you we turn with trust.

Holy Family of Nazareth,
grant that our families too
may be places of communion and prayer,
authentic schools of the Gospel
and small domestic Churches.

Holy Family of Nazareth,
may families never again
experience violence, rejection and division:
may all who have been hurt or scandalized
find ready comfort and healing.

Holy Family of Nazareth,
may the approaching Synod of Bishops
make us once more mindful
of the sacredness and inviolability of the family,
and its beauty in God's plan.

Jesus, Mary and Joseph,
graciously hear our prayer!

Amen.

Pope Francis released another prayer in 2017, more than a year before the meeting of the Synod of Bishops on young people:

Lord Jesus, in journeying toward the synod, your church
turns her attention to all the young people of the world.
We pray that they might boldly take charge of their
lives, aim for the most beautiful and profound things
of life and always keep their hearts unencumbered.
Accompanied by wise and generous guides, help them
respond to the call you make to each of them, to realize a
proper plan of life and achieve happiness.

Keep their hearts open to dreaming great dreams and
make them concerned for the good of others. Like the
Beloved Disciple, may they stand at the foot of the
Cross, to receive your Mother as a gift from you. May
they be witnesses to your Resurrection and be aware
that you are at their side as they joyously proclaim you
as Lord. Amen.

But church-sponsored events are not the only special occasions that prompt Pope Francis to compose a prayer. After visiting migrants and refugees in Lampedusa in July 2013, his second visit to an Italian city outside of Rome was to Cagliari on the island of Sardinia for a special focus on the difficult world of work and unemployment. He offered this prayer for the unemployed:

Lord God, look down upon us! Look at this city, this island. Look upon our families.

Lord, you were not without a job, you were a carpenter, you were happy.

Lord, we have no work.

The idols want to rob us of our dignity. The unjust systems want to rob us of hope.

Lord, do not leave us on our own. Help us to help each other, so that we forget our selfishness a little and feel in our heart the "we," the we of a people who want to keep on going.

Lord Jesus, you were never out of work, give us work and teach us to fight for work and bless us all. In the name of the Father, of the Son and of the Holy Spirit.

And the pope, who usually visits a cemetery for the feasts of All Souls and All Saints, decided in 2017 to remember in a special way those who died during wartime. First, he celebrated Mass at a cemetery for U.S. military who died during the World War II campaign to liberate Italy. Then he went to the Ardeatine Caves on the outskirts of Rome, where in retaliation for an attack on their troops, Nazis killed 335 men and boys, including many rounded up from Rome's Jewish neighborhood. Standing next to the chief rabbi of Rome, Pope Francis recited a prayer instead of giving a speech:

"God of Abraham, God of Isaac, God of Jacob" (cf. Ex 3:6).
With this name you presented yourself to Moses,
when you revealed to him the will to free your people
    from slavery in Egypt.
God of Abraham, God of Isaac, God of Jacob:
God who seals the covenant with man;
God who binds himself with a pact of steadfast love, for
    ever.
Merciful and compassionate
with each man and woman and with all people who
    suffer oppression.
"I have seen the affliction of my people [...] and have
    heard their cry [...]: I know their sufferings" (Ex 3:7).
God of faces and of names.
God of each of the 335 people slaughtered here on
    March 24, 1944,
whose remains rest in these graves.
You know their faces and their names.
All, even the 12 who remain unknown to us; for you no
    one is unknown.
God of Jesus, our Father who art in heaven.

Thanks to Him, the crucified and Risen One, we know
    that your name,
"God of Abraham, God of Isaac, God of Jacob,"
means that you are not God of the dead but of the living
    (cf. Mt 22:32),
that your covenant of steadfast love is mightier than
    death
and is a guarantee of resurrection.

O Lord, in this place, consecrated to the memory of
   those who have fallen for freedom and justice, let us
   divest ourselves of the trappings of selfishness and
   indifference, and through the burning bush of this
   mausoleum,
in silence, may we hear your name:
"God of Abraham, God of Isaac, God of Jacob,"
God of Jesus,
God of the living. Amen.

Peace has always been a special preoccupation of popes
and, in the last half century much of that concern has
been for peace in the Holy Land and among the Jewish,
Christian and Muslim people who live there. Standing in the
Vatican Gardens in June 2014 with the presidents of Israel
and Palestine and with Orthodox Ecumenical Patriarch
Bartholomew of Constantinople, Pope Francis led a prayer
for peace in the Holy Land:

Lord God of peace, hear our prayer!

We have tried so many times and over so many years
to resolve our conflicts by our own powers and by the
force of our arms. How many moments of hostility and
darkness have we experienced; how much blood has
been shed; how many lives have been shattered; how
many hopes have been buried . . . but our efforts have
been in vain.

Now, Lord, come to our aid! Grant us peace, teach us
peace; guide our steps in the way of peace. Open our
eyes and our hearts, and give us the courage to say:

"Never again war!"; "With war everything is lost."
Instill in our hearts the courage to take concrete steps to
achieve peace.

Lord, God of Abraham, God of the Prophets, God of
Love, you created us, and you call us to live as brothers
and sisters. Give us the strength daily to be instruments
of peace; enable us to see everyone who crosses our
path as our brother or sister. Make us sensitive to the
plea of our citizens who entreat us to turn our weapons
of war into implements of peace, our trepidation into
confident trust, and our quarreling into forgiveness.

Keep alive within us the flame of hope, so that with
patience and perseverance we may opt for dialogue
and reconciliation. In this way may peace triumph at
last, and may the words "division," "hatred," and "war"
be banished from the heart of every man and woman.
Lord, defuse the violence of our tongues and our hands.
Renew our hearts and minds, so that the word which
always brings us together will be "brother," and our way
of life will always be that of: Shalom, Peace, Salaam!

Sometimes the special occasions have a more local focus.
Outside the Basilica of St. John Lateran in November 2019,
Pope Francis dedicated a plaque commemorating all the
people who had died in the city of Rome because of poverty
and neglect. Rather than making a speech, he read a prayer:

For the millions of children bent by pangs of hunger
who have lost their smile but still want to love.

For the millions of young people who, without any
reason to believe or to live, search in vain for a future in
this senseless world.

Father, we beseech you to send workers into
your harvest.

For the millions of men, women and children whose
hearts still beat strongly enough to fight, whose spirit
rises up against the unjust destiny imposed on them,
whose courage demands the right to invaluable dignity.

Father, we beseech you to send workers into your harvest.

For the millions of children, women and men who do
not want to curse, but rather to love and pray, work
and unite so that a more solidary earth may be born;
An earth, our earth, where every man gives the best of
himself before he dies.

Father, we beseech you to send workers into
your harvest

For all those who pray, may they be listened to by God,
and receive from him the strength to eliminate misery
from a humanity made in his image.

Father, we beseech you to send workers into
your harvest.

As the coronavirus pandemic spread across the globe, bringing sickness and death, quarantines and lockdowns, unemployment and mourning, Pope Francis repeatedly offered

prayers and suggested prayers for Catholics to recite. Ahead of a day of prayer and fasting for the end of the COVID-19 pandemic in March 2020, he offered this prayer:

O Mary,
You shine continuously on our journey
as a sign of salvation and hope.
We entrust ourselves to you, Health of the Sick,
who, at the cross,
united with Jesus' pain,
keeping your faith firm.

You, Salvation of the Roman people,
know what we need,
and we trust that you will provide for those needs so that,
as at Cana of Galilee,
joy and celebration may return
after this moment of trial.

Help us, Mother of Divine Love,
to conform ourselves to the will of the Father
and to do what Jesus tells us.
He who took our suffering upon himself,
and burdened himself with our sorrows
to bring us, through the cross,
to the joy of Resurrection. Amen.

With the pandemic still raging, he wrote a letter to all Catholics, including the prayer from the day of fasting as well as a second prayer he composed for Catholics to recite in the month of May, a month traditionally dedicated to Mary:

"We fly to your protection, O Holy Mother of God."

In the present tragic situation, when the whole world is prey to suffering and anxiety, we fly to you, Mother of God and our Mother, and seek refuge under your protection.

Virgin Mary, turn your merciful eyes towards us amid this coronavirus pandemic. Comfort those who are distraught and mourn their loved ones who have died, and at times are buried in a way that grieves them deeply. Be close to those who are concerned for their loved ones who are sick and who, in order to prevent the spread of the disease, cannot be close to them. Fill with hope those who are troubled by the uncertainty of the future and the consequences for the economy and employment.

Mother of God and our Mother, pray for us to God, the Father of mercies, that this great suffering may end and that hope and peace may dawn anew. Plead with your divine Son, as you did at Cana, so that the families of the sick and the victims be comforted, and their hearts be opened to confidence and trust.

Protect those doctors, nurses, health workers and volunteers who are on the frontline of this emergency and are risking their lives to save others. Support their heroic effort and grant them strength, generosity and continued health.

Be close to those who assist the sick night and day, and to priests who, in their pastoral concern and fidelity to the Gospel, are trying to help and support everyone.

Blessed Virgin, illumine the minds of men and women engaged in scientific research, that they may find effective solutions to overcome this virus.

Support national leaders, that with wisdom, solicitude and generosity they may come to the aid of those lacking the basic necessities of life and may devise social and economic solutions inspired by farsightedness and solidarity.

Mary Most Holy, stir our consciences, so that the enormous funds invested in developing and stockpiling arms will instead be spent on promoting effective research on how to prevent similar tragedies from occurring in the future.

Beloved Mother, help us realize that we are all members of one great family and to recognize the bond that unites us, so that, in a spirit of fraternity and solidarity, we can help to alleviate countless situations of poverty and need. Make us strong in faith, persevering in service, constant in prayer.

Mary, Consolation of the afflicted, embrace all your children in distress and pray that God will stretch out his all-powerful hand and free us from this terrible pandemic, so that life can serenely resume its normal course.

To you, who shine on our journey as a sign of salvation and hope, do we entrust ourselves, O Clement, O Loving, O Sweet Virgin Mary. Amen.

But there were other special events in 2020 as well, including the fifth anniversary of his encyclical *Laudato Si'*. For the occasion, Pope Francis released a "Common Prayer for Earth and for Humanity."

Loving God,
Creator of Heaven, Earth, and all therein contained.
Open our minds and touch our hearts,
so that we can be part of creation, your gift.

Be present to those in need in these difficult times,
    especially the poorest and most vulnerable.
Help us to show creative solidarity as we confront the
    consequences of the global pandemic.
Make us courageous in embracing the changes required
    to seek the common good.
Now more than ever, may we all feel interconnected and
    interdependent.

Enable us to succeed in listening and responding to the
    cry of the Earth and the cry of the poor.
May their current sufferings become the birth-pangs of
    a more fraternal and sustainable world.

We pray through Christ our Lord, under the loving gaze
    of Mary Help of Christians.

Amen.

On the 100th anniversary of the birth of St. John Paul II—May 19, 2020—Pope Francis suggested a prayer seeking the late pope's intercession, echoing frequent refrains in the teaching and preaching of his predecessor:

Intercede so that we may always remain faithful to the Gospel.

Intercede so that we may know how to open wide the doors to Christ.

Intercede so that in these difficult times we may be witnesses of joy and mercy.

Intercede so that we may know how to respond to the needs of our brothers and sisters who suffer, recognizing in their faces, the Face of the Lord.

Help us with your intercession not to allow ourselves to be robbed of hope, and to be men and women who journey in the certainty of faith.